DEAR FEAR

Volume 4

*Powerful Lessons on Living Your Best
Life On The Other Side of Fear*

Tiana Patrice

Copyright @ 2020 by Tiana Patrice and
The Fearless Experience

All rights reserved.
No part of this publication may be reproduced, distributed, or transmitted in any form or by any means, including photocopying, recording, or other electronic or mechanical methods, without the prior written permission of the publisher, except in the case of brief quotations embodied in critical reviews and certain other noncommercial uses permitted by copyright law. For permission requests, write to the publisher, addressed "Attention: Permissions Coordinator," at the address below.

Tiana Patrice

assistant@tianapatrice.com

Ordering Information:

Quantity sales: Special discounts are available on quantity purchases by corporations, associations, and nonprofits. For details, contact the publisher at the address above.

Published by KLC Publishing

Cover Designed By The BXperience

Trigger warning: Some stories feature accounts of verbal and physical abuse

This book is intended to empower you and help you heal on the other side of fear. Its goal is to give you hope and position you for purpose. This book is not intended to provide financial, mental, health, legal advice, or any advice where professional counsel is necessary. Please seek the appropriate counsel for these matters.

TABLE OF CONTENTS:

A Message From The Visionary Author 2

Dear Fear, You Can't Have My Elevation 7

Dear Fear, You Can't Have My Promised Place 16

Dear Fear, You Can't Have My Family 30

Dear Fear, You Can't Have My Confidence 42

Dear Fear, Thank You For Making Me Shine 57

Dear Fear, You Can't Have My Purpose 82

Dear Fear, I Survived It! 96

Dear Fear, You Can't Have My Future 109

Dear Fear, You Can't Nullify My Forgiveness 119

Dear Fear, You Can't Have My Perseverance 133

Dear Fear, You Can't STOP My Healing 139

FOR GOD HATH NOT GIVEN US THE SPIRIT OF FEAR; BUT OF POWER, AND OF LOVE, AND OF A SOUND MIND.

-2 Timothy 1:7
KJV

Dear Fear

A Message from the Visionary Author

Tiana Patrice

Hello fear LESS Leader,

Welcome to the Global Book Series, Dear Fear. We are so excited to have you on this journey with us. Dear Fear is more than just a book. It's a ministry on the move designed to help you identify the spirit of fear, and make it bow in the name of Jesus. It's a tool for your transformation and success and encouragement for you to dream bigger than you've ever dreamt. Our goal is for you to take the strategies given and take immediate action against your fear. To date, we have launched more than 60 authors, whose stories have transformed lives all over the world, and we have no plans of stopping anytime soon. (Insert Praise Break)

Within the pages of this book, you will find courageous letters & stories from women leaders who decided to use their voice to help the voiceless, and use their pain to push purpose. These women stood up to the fear of their past and dethroned pride and shame to boldly step into their destiny. Was it easy? No. Necessary? Absolutely.

To every reader, my prayer for you is that you open your eyes, ears, and heart and embrace each story, each recollection, and each heartfelt letter that dethrones the power of fear. My prayer is that you see yourself in these stories and that you find the courage to share your story too.

As you read the truths inside of this book, you may come face to face with your past. I encourage you to recognize it, confront it, talk about it, and fear less.

To every author. I want to say, thank you. Thank you for believing in this movement. Thank you for trusting this platform as a safe place. Thank you for sharing your story for not only your healing but to heal and transform others. This book will shift conversations, and break generational cycles that have plagued families for years. This is only the beginning...and it has begun.

    With Love,

    Tiana Patrice

TIANA PATRICE

Dear Fear,

It's time you and I had a more recent conversation. As the Visionary Author of this book, it's easy for me to help others heal, deal, and be set free, which means it's also easy for me to hide my own issues with you. You knew that it was important for me to show face and show up for my clients. You knew that I would never let anyone see me crack, break, or be dented. You knew that my brand meant so much to me that I would allow you to punk me, beat me, and abuse me behind the scenes, and I would mask it all with a smile. However, if I must be honest, fear, you weren't my trickster. The reality is we were in it together. I knew you were there. I recognized, identified, and mapped you out. But we had a deal, and you kept your end of the bargain, and I kept mine.

Until the divorce happened.

God had my undivided attention. Not my business. Not my brand. I needed my Father. It was in those moments that I realized I couldn't fake it any longer. I couldn't hide anymore. I didn't care what they saw or what they said. I was broken. I was dented. I was afraid. I was wounded. Not from the divorce, but from all of the unhealed wounds that you convinced me to cover. But God wanted more for me. He was calling me to greater and some things had to go. He exposed me to me. In my weakest form, my God flexed his muscles for me. You had convinced me that my weakness was a weakness. My Father reminded me that it's only in my weakness that He can show off his strength. I learned to surrender, submit, and trust God. I had to address the wounds and heal. I had to identify the echoes and lies that you told me, and I had to replace them with the truth. Fear you even sent me a message in my divorce, saying "she'd never tell it, she cares too much about her brand". You forgot one thing. God is the author and finisher of my faith, and it is Him that holds the pen of my deliverance.

With that being said, fear, not only am I going to tell it....but I'm going to tell it all. My story makes hell nervous, but it gives God glory! And fear, it's the glory for me.

Healed & Whole,

Tiana Patrice.

Dear Fear,
You Can't Have My Elevation

Read My Lips

I. Don't. Want. You.

It was August 20, 2019.

Those words played over and over like a broken record, chopped, screwed and rejected. There I was standing in the doorway of a borrowed bedroom, him lying in bed, 25 days after the bottom of our marriage fell out. I stood there with tears in my eyes, begging my ex-husband for counseling. Begging him to get in the ring. Begging him to stay. Begging him to try. Begging to fix the very thing, that I didn't break. Yet there I was, standing in the ring taking blow, after blow, trying to catch my breath.

"I thought I wanted you…but I don't." Blow.

"Why would I want counseling…I'm not happy here." Blow.

"I'm not staying anywhere that I don't want to be…I want out." Knock Out.

That day I left the ring, alone, gloves off, I had no more fight… I left feeling hopeless, defeated, undeniably broken and unaccepting of the facts.

The cute but broken thing was no more.

The reality is, *sometimes it takes for the bottom to fall out of the very thing you were never designed to stand in.* #Message Sometimes it takes a hard fall, an ugly blow, a complete knock out, for you to fall to the feet of Jesus. It's in these moments that you realize, the life you validated, protected, awarded, created a covenant with, and gloated about was active, yet producing tirelessly on dry ground. It's in these moments that you truly understand the definition of being a public success, yet a private failure. Yet even in these moments, God's grace is sufficient.

Much like the story of Hannah in *1st Samuel Chapter 1*, God revealed areas in my life that had to be shut down and exposed before elevation could occur. Many times, we believe the exposure is for the adjacent party when in reality it's us that will have to navigate the spotlight of truth. That spotlight comes with ugly realizations and rugs that are woven together by generational lies, cycles, and curses.

In 1st Samuel, we find Hannah burdened with grief because God had shut her womb. In the old testament days, it was a shame and a disgrace for women to be barren because the value of a woman was placed on her ability to produce seed. Interestingly enough in our society, we have idealistic views on education, producing children, marriage, and many other things that characterize who we are. We buy into the idea that marriage is to serve the opinions of others and our self-absorbing beliefs, vs to serve God's purpose and agenda.

My exposure came from giving in to these views with impure motives and the idea of finding completeness in a marriage. For 10 years I created an idol out of the idea of marriage in a relationship that while it had its great times, was never assigned to the woman God created me to be. My hunger in these seasons wasn't after Christ, but after a title that I didn't even understand the concept of. Because of this, I married a season and tried to make it a lifetime.

Whew Chilllleeeeee! It's something about when God does the exposing. Baby the rug will have to be burned! You see, I believed marriage would make me "somebody". I thought being married would make others take me seriously. I lived in the fantasy of having a complete home, with the father of my child. I paraded in the lights of having it all "together". I believed marriage would make up for my past mistakes, and right my wrongs.

Having the child out of wedlock would be ok now. Wouldn't it?

Staying in the 10 year relationship was worth it now. Wasn't it?

Finally, I could prove I wasn't stupid for staying and waiting, I finally got my ring...Ironically, the same ring I begged for, was the same ring I had to walk away from when my exposure came.

How many of you can relate with this?

Willing to live a lifestyle outside of the will of God, because of your insecurities, fears, and voids. Willing to ignore the signs, because you convinced yourself that it would get better. Willing to stay with "comfortable" because you didn't fully believe in *Jeremiah 29:11*, and the plans God has for your life.

Believe me when I say...I certainly can relate.

Here is my encouragement to you. Right now, at this moment, do a complete self-evaluation…. even if it hurts. Ask yourself, what am I holding onto because I'm afraid to find out what life is like without it. For some of you it's fear, for some it's your past hurts and pains, for some it's relationships and connections with people. Whatever it is, I urge you to take it to God and ask him to chisel, prune, and pluck anything in you and around you that doesn't line up with His plan for your life. Why? Because in this season of your life, you are too old, grown, and called for anything that is cute and broken. Period.

The very next day I was scheduled for a mammogram for a breast cancer scare which was the turning point of this story. I was alone at the hospital, and being moved from room to room with doctors around, whispering about their findings. As I laid back on the cold table being pushed, mushed and everything in between, I heard the Lord say, *"Don't try to keep a door open that is being closed by me"* (whew Chile, somebody needed to hear that)

In that moment, I knew this was NOT the fight God ever intended for me.

I realized that God connected me with the story of Hannah, not because I needed a new word to share or another inspirational quote, but because he wanted to show me what he could do with a barren place. Using Hannah, God gave me a perfect blueprint of how to get to my breakthrough, before I even knew I would be broken. (And now, I get to share this blueprint with you.)

When I left the hospital, I left with a praise break, the cysts were benign! I also left encouraged with new strength. It was time to let God be God. That day I got back in the ring, but this time was different. I didn't get in the ring alone or broken. I got back in the ring with God by my side. I put my gloves back on.

This war was personal.

It wasn't about my ex-husband. It was about what God wanted to do with me and through me. I walked back to the doorway of that borrowed bedroom, I looked my ex-husband in the eyes, and I boldly said: "I stand in agreement with you. I want the divorce" It was time to begin the journey of crushing the old me, for the new woman to emerge.

What decisions or situations have you placed yourself in because of fear?

_____

_____

_____

_____

Healing requires complete honesty. What were the REAL reasons you made those decisions and how can you break the cycle now?

Dear Fear

_____

_____

_____

_____

CHEMICKA THOMPSON

Dear Fear,

I must inform you that you are no longer needed here. You must pack your bags and leave. I know, I know, your presence has been faithful and we have been together a very long time. I know that when everyone else left, you remained. We became the best of friends you and I. You were always there to encourage me to do things I shouldn't or discourage me from doing things I should. When things went left I ran to you for comfort. You were the only one there for me to share my hurt with. You were Bonnie and I Clyde. You were easy, you were my mask, you were my excuse for the wrong I did all of those years.

That was before. Things have changed now that I found the love I needed. The love of Jesus. I realize I no longer need you because I am needed on the other side of you. **I will fulfill my purpose.** You have delayed me long enough. I have things to do and places to go. Fear, this is farewell. You have to exit now because I have a new rider. Her name is Hope. The two of us are headed to freedom, and fear, you are not welcome there.

Signed,

Unmasked-Unafraid

Chemicka Thompson

Dear Fear, You Can't Have My Promised Place

Have you ever felt like all was lost? Your will power, lost. Your strength, lost. Your mind, lost. I have, and it was not pretty. I want to take some time to take you on a journey. This journey, like many, has its ups and downs, but in the end, fear lost, and God got the glory.

I came from a two-parent home in a good neighborhood with good friends and love from a big family. I had a good childhood despite the bumps that came later down the road. My younger self enjoyed life, and for the most part, I was happy. Things changed for me when I entered Jr. High. I noticed that I was different from the other girls, and instead of using my voice, I hid my feelings. It all started with the laughs around my clothing, and it seemed to never end. You see, my Grandfather and Grandmother took pride in shopping for us at Kmart and Sears. I loved those shopping trips. I would carefully dress in the new clothes and head off to school. I learned that what I thought was great, others made jokes about. "You look homely" my classmates would say. I was devastated. This caused me to question who I was at a very young age, and was the start of my image issues. I would try to stick to my real friends, the ones who didn't care how I dressed. The ones that would come play with me in the yard after school because they knew that I was sad from being picked on. After a while, their consoling no longer worked. It wasn't long before my unhappiness transformed into its own behavior.

Around the age of 15 that behavior changed my life. I grew up way too fast. I saw the teenage me, the one who loved playing jump rope and hopscotch change drastically. I was no longer a happy teenager. I was angry and lonely. Today, I wish I had made better choices, but I was sad. Realizing that I did not fit in at home or school, I began to put myself in places I shouldn't have. I allowed people to take advantage of my brokenness that should have never had access to me. My actions at the moment held no consequence. I was filling voids and looking for love. I did not know the damage that I was doing. But then...I started feeling sick.

My mother took me to the doctor, and after many appointments and tests, the doctor determined that I was suffering from the Sickle Cell trait. It got worse each week and it was decided I would home school. It wasn't long before I realized, this was not just Sickle Cell. After speaking with a friend, I knew the truth, I was pregnant. I was beyond afraid. I had no idea what to do or say. I was sick every day, and the doctors had missed this. Every day I laid there in silence, sadness, and shame. My baby grew, and so did my fear, but I stuck with the doctor diagnosis. Until I could no longer hide it, it was time to have my baby.

Coming home from the hospital with a healthy baby girl I did not know what to feel. I had no idea what to do either. I was overwhelmed and my senior year of high school was starting in 5 weeks! I was skeptical about returning but knew I had to. Especially now. I have my daughter to care for. I was embarrassed yet proud as a Mother. I was excited at the opportunity to see my friends but nervous about the obvious conversation starter. I was still extremely sad as well; I now know it is called postpartum depression. I had more questions than answers. I mean no one even knew I was pregnant until 5 days before I delivered. At one of my sickle cell appointments, it was discovered. I believe my Mother finally asked for the test because it sure looked like I was pregnant. There was no time to plan what I would do after birth. No time to buy a crib or diapers. One night I was a teenager, and the next day I was a teenage mom.

Those 5 days before delivery were the worst. It came with all the accusations, ugly words, and stares. I may have been able to ignore it from strangers, but from home I cannot describe the number of tears I shed. Hearing my Mother cry at night made me want to be invisible. This shifted quickly because everyone's attention was now on the new bundle of joy.for the most part. I smiled and tried to adapt and learn quickly so that they could at least say I was doing my best. On the inside I was crying **I NEED HELP.** I was not brave enough to say it though. I was waiting for someone to say that it will be ok. I was waiting for someone to say you can do this. That wasn't my reality. I only heard negative comments and no encouragement. I felt guilty, like an inconvenience. When the family came over to visit, they would come with questions about my future and unwanted suggestions. My Mother was just as confused as I was. She was just as embarrassed as I was. She was scared too. Our eyes would lock during conversations like these. She was afraid of her life and I was afraid of what life would now be. "I am sorry Mama" is all I could muster to say.

This pushed me even harder to finish my Senior year. My friends gave me hope. They did not act like I was a failure. My life had changed and even though I wanted to hang out with my friends I wanted to graduate more. My daily mantra was "I will not fail. I am so close. I will graduate from high school." I was an emotional mess, yet determined. The constant outside reminders of "You are not going to be able to graduate with that baby" fueled a fire in me. I would prove "them" wrong. "Them" being the people I thought loved me most. Being told these things to my face was meant to break me. It started building me. Adds to the mantra, I WILL show them!

As far back as I can remember I was involved in church. I carried my baby girl to church, dressed in pink ruffles and bows, with all the pride of a new mother. The tension and stares almost choked me in service. On the ride home I cried. Grandmother sat in the car quietly and let me cry. We sat outside of my house until the tears dried up. She would say that it is just unacceptable to have a child out of wedlock. This was coming from the woman who made sure for many years that I wore the right color stocking on the right Sunday and that my skirts were past my knees and that I wore a slip under my dresses...she was only telling me right. Hearing it only made me cry more. Between the sobs I was able to choke out the words...I just want to finish school Granny. I just want to graduate. Finally, I used my voice.

My grandmother agreed to share babysitting duties with her Aunt Mattie. She told me I could accomplish anything that I wanted because God gives grace and mercy. She became my motivator. She wanted to prove the same thing I wanted to prove. That I am not WHAT you say I am, I am WHO God says I am. I will not be a statistic, and neither will my child. My grandmother and I bonded that very day.

Going back to school was nice. I did not have to worry about my daughter, she was being taken care of. I was able to see my friends during school hours. Outside of those 7 hours, I did not have time for friends. I managed to make it to class every day. As I got closer to the finish line I smiled more. I felt like I could make it. I would soon be able to show my friends, family, and neighbors the diploma on the wall. During the year I got closer to some of my long-time friends. I was determined to enjoy some of the Senior year with them. I wanted to go to Prom…I mean you only get one of those. There was a Senior trip, but it was costly. I decided to have a Senior sleepover and my Parents allowed it. We had a very good time. I worked on the yearbook staff, I was able to be a kid at the Pep Rallies, and went home to be a mom.

The days leading up to graduation were full of emotions. I felt great, I was nervous, I was in goal crushing mode. Plus, my 18th birthday was one month after graduation. I felt like I was sitting on top of the world. I had planned on moving for my birthday. Happy Birthday to me! I just wanted space for me and my daughter and wanted to be able to make my own decisions. Life would be much better then. or so I thought. My Mothers smile at graduation was like a ray of sunshine. More beautiful than the brightest rainbow. **I felt GREAT. I DID IT! I MADE IT!** My plans of moving came to a halt when my mother told me "You're not leaving until I get all my welfare out of you".

Life is what you make it. I had dreams and goals. I learned at an early age that I was good with my hands, so I used that to my advantage. Grandmother always told me "do not sit around waiting for a handout, find something you are good at and make your own money." By age 20 I was on my way to being a licensed cosmetologist. But life showed up. I received a phone call that changed my life again…Mom had passed away. Out of all the hospital trips before, this one was different. This one was final. Grief took over, and there I was again, scared and alone. I needed counseling. I started missing classes and lost my job. I was falling into a deep depression and the cycle started all over again. I started making bad decisions with men, some were even life-threatening. I had another child, more depression...fights, drugs...wait...this is a familiar recurring nightmare, right?

I lived without thinking or feeling for a very long time. Yet trying to fill another void. A void my grief left. Not just from my Mom passing. I was still trying to fill the void my Dad left. I needed my mother's guidance on so many things. Yes, at 20 I still needed it. A mother gives unconditional love and I had no one else. This was a very dark place and time. I got so lost in the dark that I did not recognize myself. I lived years depressed, hidden, and lost.

This persona of Chemicka went through life. I entertained; I was good at it. I sang at church, got a few dead-end jobs. When that was not enough, I stole to feed my kids. I smiled like I was not hurting. I thought if I could just keep one foot in front of the other, just keep moving, the hurt must leave, right? But when I looked in the mirror, I saw my mom's life. I had started living my mother's truth. How did I get here and How can I come out? I asked God to Help me! I knew I could go no further without God's help. I prayed and I waited. And I waited. I sat for several days, not functioning, not thinking, not feeling just waiting for something to happen.

Day 3: My boyfriend left. I watched him leave and did not feel a thing.

Day 5: My heart is hurting but that is a familiar hurt. Everyone leaves.

Day 6: Everything is hurting, my ears from the kids, my heart from loss, my body from depression.

I found enough strength to call my Grandmother. I don't even know where the lie came from. I told her I had to work the weekend and asked if she could help with the kids. She came for them and I acted normal. As soon as they drove away, I found myself swallowing pill after pill. I do not know how many I took, the bottle said to take for pain…and that is all I felt. I do not remember getting to the hospital. They pumped my stomach. I didn't know that was possible. I could not even succeed at suicide. Grandmother was contacted as my next of Kin. She took me home, set me up in her bed, and said nothing. She took care of the kids, prayed over me, and waited. Laying there I FELT SO MANY THINGS. The pain was still there, but shame had me too. I knew in this moment of my life I needed to repent. *God I am so sorry.* I had to ask for forgiveness and get my life together. I waited on God in my decisions to move at that point. He saved me because He loves me. I learned at that time that I am stronger because of the pain I have endured. God promises to never leave me, and He did not.

You have the power and strength inside of you. I felt lonely and alone, but God was always there. Seek Him. God loved me all along. No other love was greater. God's love transformed me. My mind was restored through His word. He supplied everything I longed for. He corrected my wrongs to right. And even though everyone has had their opinion, even when they laughed and plotted, me and my daughter are here. Loneliness is gone. I can trust and I can love again. I have been blessed with a husband who is patient enough and this love is peeling layers back. I am blessed with a large family to display all the love I missed. My Grandmother took me to church 3 times a week. After I no longer had my Mom, I looked to her for many things. Her unwavering Faith helped me to open my eyes and change my life. I did not know how to open my mouth and ask for help. God knew all my needs and has supplied them. Do not be afraid to open your mouth. Talk to someone you trust I wish I had. Make your decisions with God. It is the only explanation I have for making it this far and being able to share this with you. What changed me? Faith. What brought me out of depression? Hope. What saved me? Love.

And the greatest of these is love **1 Corinthians 13:13**

How will you stop fear from keeping you from your goals and dreams?

_____

_____

How will you stop allowing fear to steal your voice and silence your truth?

Bio:

Chemicka Thompson is a native of Panama City Fl, now residing in Dothan Al. She is the eldest of 3 siblings, a devoted wife to her wonderful husband and the mother to 6 wonderful children. She is a blossoming entrepreneur that's dedicated to helping women give birth safely. Her favorite hobby is enjoying nature, and reading.

MONIQUE DANZEY

Dear Fear,

You've had me longer than you should have. You made my decisions for me and even held me captive. To be honest, you even tried to scare me out of writing this letter to you. I am doing things differently now. This is my divorce decree to you. I will no longer allow you to choke the life out of me because through Jesus Christ, I have life more abundantly. You can no longer have my relationship with my father because our relationship is healed in Jesus' name! You made me think it would be impossible to have healthy relationships with my family and as of today, I speak true love, joy, and peace back into those relationships also.

I am divorcing you now so that my husband-to-be can have a whole, free, and loving wife. I am divorcing you now so that my children and their children and children to come never even know who you are. The weights you tried to place on my mind are gone now, in Jesus' name because God has not given me the spirit of fear but of power, love, and a sound mind.

I am taking my power back, the power that allows me to tread upon serpents and scorpions. I am taking the power back that gives me the authority to lay hands on the sick and see them recover! Fear you cannot have the ministry that is on the inside of me. You can't have my gifts because they belong to God. I will not allow you to place a muzzle over my mouth because I know who God has called me to be and what He has called me to do and that is to spread the gospel of Jesus Christ throughout the world. You are a liar and I will not allow you to hold me hostage anymore!!! Today is our divorce day.

Finally Free,

Monique Danzey

Dear Fear, You Can't Have My Family

Do you know what they say about preachers' kids? They say that we are the worst ones. They say that we do everything under the sun. They even say that we aren't as perfect as we seem. Well let me tell you something...it's all true. I wish I could paint a story that was as perfect as the lifestyle may have portrayed, but the reality is...I was a hot mess...and in my adulthood, I'm still recovering, forgiving, and learning my identity outside of the image.

Let's go on a journey. When I first moved to Alabama in the summer of 1998, I was the "new kid on the block". I had no friends, didn't know anyone, and barely knew my family because we only would visit during the summer for a week. This move was very difficult for me, as I wasn't given the time needed to come to terms with the move and was left to unpack my emotions on my own. Imagine learning that you were to leave everything you knew behind. Imagine leaving every laugh, every moment, every friend, every memory, because God was calling you to new territory. I was forced to end friendships and box up memories and while a part of me understood, there was another part of me that retaliated with rebellion. I was comfortable around my friends, classmates, and church family. I was hurt that I had to leave my pastor behind as well. Even though we had a big church roster, he always remembered his little Monique. That goodbye was the last time I ever saw him alive. He was one of my greatest inspirations in ministry.

The first time I can remember becoming familiar with fear was in 2nd grade. I had just transferred to a new school and while I was ready to "tackle" the year, I couldn't help but fear not being accepted and being alone. To be a child and leave a place where everything was just right only to pick up and go to a "foreign" place because God said so, was extremely frightening. I did not fully understand who God was besides the man who died for our sins, parted the Red Sea, and turned water into wine. So why would I trust a man that I could not see, feel, or even hear a response from when I prayed to him at night?

At the age of 13, I began to feel like the "black sheep". Being labeled this made me cry many days and nights because I just wanted to be a regular teenager. I felt like I was constantly being picked on because I wasn't as up to speed as most girls my age. My parents became very strict during my teenage years and at the time I did not understand it but now I know it was all for my good. I felt like I was being treated like an outsider because I chose to be the "church girl" while others chose to go down a different path. I was not given the choice on whether or not I wanted to go down this path, but even though sometimes I hated it, it also came with a lot of rewards from God. It allowed me to not be so exposed to things of the world. Yes, it meant that I was a little behind the learning curve when it came to the "streets" but there were a lot of things I am glad I didn't learn.

As I got a little older, my self-confidence began to drop tremendously. Being in the 1st family meant I always had to appear to be "perfect". I was nowhere near perfect and spent most of my teenage years trying to prove myself to everyone. I just wanted to be a regular teenager who went to the movies, skating, bowling, etc. but I couldn't because I wasn't allowed to do much. I was made to dress in a certain way and to act a particular way. I was taught to ALWAYS wear stockings in church when you wear a dress. I remember as a teenager I was going to a banquet with my father and I wore a shirt that I had ironed, but got wrinkled when I sat down while waiting on him to finish getting dressed. My father was hysterical after he saw it. We got in the car and proceeded to go to the event. Once we arrived, my dad was still mad and made me sit in the car and call my brother to come to pick me up. I felt my heart sink into my chest and I cried like a baby. This affected me in so many ways. From then on, I felt like perfection was the motive for getting dressed on Sundays. Even though this moment was one I will never forget, it taught me that God looks at my heart. Don't get me wrong, I do believe there is a standard when it comes to dressing for church but I know God wouldn't have frowned upon my semi-wrinkled shirt.

While I was in the process of getting to know myself and overcoming the feeling of being the "black sheep", I always had these particular cousins that I could always be myself around. I remember one night during the summer a few of my cousins and I were staying at my grandparent's house and I let one of them use my phone to call their boyfriend. As it got later in the night, I wanted my phone back. I asked for it and my cousin's boyfriend said, "Tell that fat girl that no one wants to talk to her so she doesn't need her phone". It didn't hurt that he said those words because I was used to that feeling. What hurt was that my cousin said absolutely nothing to defend me and it crushed my soul. I called my brother at midnight and asked him to come and get me to take me home. That was one of the most hurtful moments of my life and it completely changed my outlook on life.

I began to find a different family in my friends. My friends and I all went through similar situations with our families. They understood what it meant to be the "black sheep". My friends viewed me as Monique, not the pastor's daughter. Finally, I wasn't seen as perfect but as another individual finding their way through life. We would all hang out at each other's homes, attend church services together, and even do music with one another. I finally felt loved by "family" even though I had my real family in the same city. These friends were there for me during some of the hardest times of my life even the passing of my brother in June of 2013.

I felt like things were going to get better with my family after my brother died but they got WORST! Moments when you expect your family to gather together and love on you during that time, it was the complete opposite for my parents and me. My family became even more torn apart. When my brother died, my relationship with my father dwindled also. As if things between my dad and me weren't already chaotic, my brother's death left a void that my presence could not fill. Naturally a daddy's girl, I was left to be just a girl, figuring out life on her own. I never felt like I was good enough to simply just be his child and that hurt. Don't get me wrong, my dad is a wonderful man but there are moments that I wished he would be the father he was to me when I was younger.

I used to struggle in such a way with forgiving all of them for the pain and hurt they had caused me throughout the years, but I learned that I had to forgive them to be free! Who would have thought the pastor's kid had issues with forgiving people? Well, I did, but God helped me through it all. Getting to my place of freedom wasn't so easy. Many days I couldn't put my feelings into words so all I could do was cry my eyes out. Some days were filled with malice and hatred, but I had to learn how to give that over to God. During this process, I learned what Nehemiah 8:10, "the joy of the Lord is my strength" meant. I exchanged my weakness for His strength and my sorrows for His joy. This also meant that I had to be real with myself. All the things I tried to hide under my smile and "title" had to be uncovered. I could no longer hide things under the rug but I had to deal with them and heal from them in order to be able to walk into my new season.

The new Monique is healed, whole, and made free! On the day after my brother's birthday in 2020, I sent text messages to my sister in law, nephew, and niece apologizing for any wrong that I had done. Little did I know, my healing was waiting on me the whole time. After sending the text messages, they all responded the same way...they had been wanting to mend our broken relationships too. That made my heart smile and I felt a 7-year-old weight lift off of my back. I could finally breathe again!

Freedom is on the other side of my fear and I am loving the way it feels. Being free of these things that held me captive as a child has given me great insight. My confidence has been taken to another level because I had to learn that no one can love me better than myself. My relationship with my dad is a work in progress, and I never realized it until now but my dad was only trying to protect me in ministry. While the minister of music was trying to shut me up, he was teaching me how to worship in spirit and in truth. He taught me to still give God glory no matter what others were trying to throw my way. To his defense, it is impossible for a person to "fix" something if they never knew it was broken. We are well on our way to the bond we once had when I was a little girl. I simply explained to my father that I did not want to create a generational curse because I refused to take it into my marriage. Even though it was a little hard for him to come to grips with my truth, he understood and is now willing to do the work.

Freedom is not free, it costs. It cost me quite a bit but what I gained in return was well worth the process and there's so much more to tap into. Living in my truth and learning how to overcome some of the "ugly" truth has made me dig deep into places I never really intended on digging in. The "ugly" truth has made me cry late at night, angry, and even want to give up but I knew I had to continue on my journey to get to my destination of freedom.

What family issues have you swept under the rug that has held you from walking in your destiny?

_____

_____

_____

_____

What plan do you have in place to help you deal and heal from your past family trauma?

_____

_____

_____

_____

BIO:

Monique Nicole Danzey is a gifted soul that entered this world on August 10, 1990 to Reverend Norris and Lady Laura Danzey. She hails from the home town of Virginia Beach, VA. During her young age, Monique began to see an amazing gift be produced and she began singing in her church's youth choir. At 7 years old, she sang her first solo entitled "Silver and Gold"; by Kirk Franklin. Through this humble beginning, a passion for God and His word was formed which increased her love for music in a greater way. It was by this that Monique began to lead a life of worship and submission to the spirit of God and gained access to Him at an early age. The Danzey family later relocated to Dothan, AL and this was only the beginning of her ministry as she knows it now. Monique was a member of the Wiregrass Choral Society from 2002-2008 under the direction of Derrick Duncan. Currently, Monique serves faithfully as a praise team member at Hines Chapel AME in Dothan, AL. Her Gift is submitted to her pastor, Apostle Paul Horn. Currently, God has blessed Monique to birth two singles; "Greater is He" and "Use Me", which were both given to her through prayer and consecration. "Use Me" was released on August 12, 2017 and she is currently working to release new music very soon.

CYNTHIA C. FARMER

Dear Fear,

Your grip may have paralyzed me from an early age muting my voice for decades and taking away my confidence, but your reach ends here. As I've grown fearless, you've become powerless! You have no authority over me any longer and I vow to eradicate your grip across the nations! Voices will be heard, warriors will rise up against you, and generational cycles will be destroyed. Fear, you have no place in this kingdom agenda and you will bow! The power in my voice will bring breakthrough to my nation, and it starts today!

For too long, I've given you power over me and let you reign over every decision I made throughout life, big and small. So many life-altering decisions were made in hopes that people would see me as strong and successful—that I would be accepted. No matter what, you made sure the world expressed how I still wasn't enough. Three degrees, a husband, three beautiful children, a home, and multiple businesses later, you still, somehow, managed to convince me that I wasn't enough—that my life was not worth living and that I should just end it all. I cried, I screamed, I fought demons in these dark moments, but I chose to live. I live and I'm living.

I believe in the truth and the power of the living Word of the true and living God. I shall live and not die! It shall all come together for my good!

A part of me thanks you for the role you played. That's the perfect word, too: "played," because you certainly got played thinking you were playing me. Yes, I can recall every insult ever spewed at me and I can play them like a record on repeat, the melody of the opinions of others playing out in my mind. Yes, I spent time reinventing myself over and over again just to be liked and accepted. And yes, I didn't know who I was; I didn't know who God created me to be. But that's where you messed up: the day you pushed a little too hard, forcing me down on my knees in the perfect position to cry out to God, be heard, and hear HIS voice! At that moment, God spoke into my spirit and said "I, the almighty creator of heaven and earth, created you! You are my beloved and you are my greatest work yet! I've given you authority and anointing in your voice. Speak daughter! Rise up and be the warrior I created you to be! Raise up the kingdom warriors with your voice! You are enough!" By the time I rose back up to my feet, it was too late for you, you were already defeated. Goodbye, fear.

Signed off,

Cynthia C. Farmer

Dear Fear, You Can't Have My Confidence

I remember the day I threw it all away and turned my back on the person *they* wanted me to be, the person I spent decades creating. She was shattered. I was shattered. The shell of my exterior that I created to keep the hurt, pain, love, and joy of others away from me came to a shattering end. In all reality, it was false protection against an enemy that was actually and always inside, never outside. Come with me for a moment and stop what you're doing and feel, not just read this, but feel what I felt in that moment of shattering: the screaming, the shouting, the crying, the crying out, then dropping to my knees, the heavy tears and silent tears crying out to God—Help! God, I need you! It hurts, everything hurts-- it's too heavy and I can't carry this anymore! Head hung low, with a faded, quiet sob, I mustered up enough strength to whisper one more time "Jesus, help me please…" What finally shattered me completely? It was the day I found out that the **spirits of abandonment and rejection had taken up residence in my marriage.** And while I wish my story started there, it doesn't. I also thank God that it doesn't end there either.

For decades, I carried around this figurative suitcase filled to the brim with things God never intended for me to carry. This suitcase was filled with things like abandonment, rejection, fear, self-consciousness, and the like. I consciously and subconsciously packed for "just in case" and "what ifs;" Just in case they're mean to me, just in case they don't like me, just in case they judge me, just in case they reject me. I stayed packed and ready. No one could hurt me or ever leave me before I hurt or left them. My shell was tough. Much like a crab, my exterior available to the world to see and judge was hard yet beautiful and intricate. It could withstand the attacks of the world yet it was beautiful enough to stop onlookers dead in their tracks, giving off the appearance of a bold confidence and unmatched strength. Can you relate? I lived and operated in the shell. No one knew the soft, weak, and highly unstable interior that the shell protected. On the inside, words and opinions cut deep to the core, and my spirit could literally get eaten alive by those things. I was a slave, in bondage by the opinions of others. So badly I wanted to be liked, loved, and accepted. I think back over the foolish and even dangerous things I did just to be acknowledged and praised, no matter the costs. My attention-seeking ranged from making honor roll, being a captain of the dance team, and being the president or vice president of every organization I joined—and trust me, there were many organizations I joined. The acts continued into self-harming thoughts for attention, and promiscuous decisions just to fit in. If only I knew back then what I know now—that I wasn't created to fit in and that my life experiences weren't there to break me, but to prepare me for the calling on my life. Being broken into position isn't being broken, it's simply being positioned.

So where did it all begin? Let me get you up to speed. My bondage to the opinions of others entered when I was only 2 years old. One thing I've come to learn is that the devil has no limits or age restrictions! He hits below the belt, kicks you when you're down, adds insult to injury and doesn't think twice about it. Trust me when I say, you're never too young to get attacked. The attacks launched against me at a very early age were purposeful and strategic. I had to learn that the enemy wasn't just after me and my confidence, but my destiny and the people connected to that destiny.

My mother and father divorced when I was 2 and I was never taught the difference between goodbye and see you later. I thought my dad left us, I thought he didn't want us. Every departure in life felt like an intense and overwhelming experience of abandonment. I felt it every time family was visiting and would leave. I felt it every time a friend had to go home. I felt it over and over again. I felt like I was abandoned so many times, it was easy to leave, yet I was stuck. I was stuck at 3 years old where I can remember my dad coming to visit with the biggest doll I had ever seen and told me he couldn't stay. I was stuck at 8 years on that hill near my house when that girl said "why do you talk like that? You talk like a white girl!" in such an inquisitive yet condescending tone. I got stuck at 18 years old where I was judged by my peers even though I adopted their persona, they found other ways to dislike me and marginalize me. I got stuck at 31 years old when I lost everything I used to create my shell of confidence. This "stuck" was different though. This "stuck" was my rock bottom.

Ignoring your feelings does not heal them. Unhealed trauma will seep out in very unhealthy ways. It was never explained to me that my parents' divorce was not a reflection of my father's love for me. It wasn't until that spirit of abandonment reared its ugly head in my marriage that I decided to have a sit down with my father to learn the truth. I needed to be set free so that I could destroy the generational curse that was trying to destroy my marriage and my children. For me, it was time to get unstuck—I needed my healing and my deliverance. "Did you not love me enough to stay? Was I not good enough? Did I do something wrong?" These questions shaped who I was in everything I did. I chased down acceptance! I wanted to be everything everyone needed. I thought: then, everyone would like me, love me, and never leave me! In striving to be perfect, I never acknowledged my faults, which played a huge part in my inability to accept constructive criticism, brush off insults, and heal effectively. It caused me to be clingy in friendships and relationships which played a part in some people leaving me. I internalized everything and had no confidence. In my mind, perfection was the only success—a detrimental mindset to have.

Quickly, as if to spit it out before I changed my mind, I said to my father in a demanding tone "why did you leave us? Why did you divorce my mom? I am struggling in my marriage and I'm hurt from you abandoning us!" For a moment, he didn't say anything. What followed the brief silence shocked me. I could hear the hurt in his voice. I heard a tone that I had never heard before. The pain that came through in his voice shocked me, it shook me. These questions that I answered for myself over the years were destroying me and I needed my dad to help restore me. My father told me he didn't abandon me. He fought to stay. He even battled with the police to stay and the police advised him that it would be best for him to leave. The police??? You, a black immigrant, fought against the police in New York, the NYPD, circa 1989, for me? That was so far from the answers I was given and the answers I gave myself. He began to tell me the account of their marriage, reliving a dark and painful era of his life. His truth set me free—mostly.

When I hit rock bottom, my hurt and anger now turned towards God. Lord, why would you allow all of this to happen to me? Why? I prayed earnestly and received answers and prophecies that this was the path He chose for me to walk. A path that would break me into a million pieces! What kind of God are you? Do you want to punish me for every sin I've ever committed? Well, you've done it. I didn't talk to God for two weeks (where I normally talk to him multiple times a day). I cried daily. I felt pain everywhere—emotional, spiritually, physically. Still, I asked God what I should do. Should I stay in my marriage or should I leave? Should I run from it all or tough it out? God, should I live or should I die?

In this place, I struggled to love myself. I struggled to love God, and I contemplated suicide. I blamed myself for my rock bottom. During the day, I kept myself together for the kids but during the night, I sobbed myself to sleep. I hated my husband. I hated myself. I hated God. God began to use everything around me to minister to my broken heart. If I wouldn't go to Him, He made sure He came to me. It took me two weeks but I finally prayed and listened. Lord, what do I do? Do I stay or do I go, and whatever the answer, how do I do it? God brought it to remembrance, that spirit I saw rising against my marriage and my household during a time of prayer. Yes, demonic spirits are real, but so is Jehovah Gabor, the god who wars for you. Warring in this instance was the ability to effectively communicate and to hear what the spirit was saying. Healthy and effective communication is powerful, necessary, transformative, sustaining, and healing.

When God spoke and I listened, He said "Daughter, I need you to live!" But how Lord? God answered, "with me and through me." So much hurt and pain, I screamed out, Lord, show me, me! How did I get here? How do I leave this place? How do I keep living? I felt rejected because I thought my dad left us. I felt abandoned when he said he couldn't stay. I felt rejected when that girl asked me why I spoke that way. I felt depressed and worthless when I got my heart broken and shattered. How Lord? That's when I had to make the choice for myself: to live and not die. *God, I choose to live! Show me how.* I felt empowered when I made the decision to live after *all* of this. I decided to give God my full yes, which included accepting my father's truth, forgiving the girl on the hill, releasing my peers from college, and forgiving my husband and staying, giving everyone the same love, grace, and mercy that I expect from God daily. I prayed and cried and talked a lot! I sought wise counsel and aired everything out. My husband and I devoted our marriage back to God and he gave me the grace to talk everything through, even if it was redundant. My husband gave me the grace and space to hurt and to heal, watching helplessly knowing he could not be the one to heal me. So instead, he also gave God his full yes, and devoted himself to being all who God called him to be. Our journey to us, indeed, requires its own chapter and will be revealed in full one day, but we are a testament to what happens when you give God your full yes! I cannot fully explain the love and confidence I have for myself today, just me, through Christ. Not my titles, my degrees, my accomplishments, my husband, nor my income—just me. I'm a better wife and mother because of it, because of Christ. Truly, all things work for the good of those who love Christ and your love lies in your yes; your obedience.

So what do I want to leave with you? My reality was that for my entire life, I created confidence based on successes; external things that were not sustainable. I was never confident in myself. I built a life that my parents could be proud of, always strived for the higher salary, drove the luxury car, married tall, dark, and sexy, served in church, remained obedient to Christ and got the half-million dollar home. I had built a beautiful life, family, and career. Yet, I didn't love me. I wasn't confident in myself. Abandonment and rejection led to my seeking of outward validation and acceptance. All of that was because I never gave God my full "yes." I had a bold relationship with him up to a certain extent. I trusted Christ with my life, my marriage, children, finances, and ministry, but I didn't trust him with my worth. Placing your worth in man will leave you worthless. My rock bottom was my opportunity; the time was nigh to give Him all of me, inside and out. It was time to get into my seat of power and authority! It was always mine to have. I had to release the spirits of fear and unforgiveness that were holding me back from the kingdom, and I had to learn to love through my pain and healing. It was time to be the warrior that I was created to be-- the force that the enemy wanted no parts of! Look, we have always been more powerful than we know. Long before we were a thought in our parents' mind, we were conceived in the heart of God! If that won't make you shout, then I don't know what will!

The moment we allow the love, light, and power of Christ to shine through our lives is the moment we say yes to a bold confidence in ourselves through Christ and even bolder confidence in Christ himself. We are such powerful beings, and when we are walking in our calling, purpose, and power, the kingdom is unstoppable and souls are saved and set free! You are more powerful, gifted, and anointed than you think, and sis, you haven't even begun to scratch the surface. If there is nothing else I've done here, let it be that I spoke to the warrior within who is beginning to get stirred up. Because it's not a matter of if, it's a matter of when. War is inevitable, but so is winning. Be confident in this very thing, that you were created for the battles you are facing. Lay your confidence safely in the hands of Jesus, and watch him work! Thankfully, the only place to go from rock bottom is up.

Think about some of your biggest, most obvious fears. What deeper fear is your *obvious* fear based in?

_____

_____

_____

_____

Think about each of your fears and evaluate if it's realistic. Are your fears rational, logical, factual, and true?

Dear Fear

_____
_____
_____
_____

Bio:

Cynthia C. Farmer is a wife to a loving husband, mother of 3 amazing boys, preacher, speaker, author, and CEO. At an early age, Cynthia's voice was muted by incessant insults, often by those of her peers, and began to battle with the spirits of abandonment and rejection. Throughout life, she's fought to love all of her, but particularly her voice, both literally and figuratively. It wasn't until Cynthia was unexpectedly placed in ministry that she had to face her world-created fear head on, only to discover her God-given purpose and passion: Speaking!

Although full of joy and success, warfare has been a regular part of Cynthia's life and therefore, so has prayer. Throughout life, Cynthia has experienced many trials: some warfare and some self-inflicted. She's experienced insecurities, anxiety, depression, heartbreaks and soul ties, near death experiences, pregnancy and infant loss, joblessness, financial hardship, suddenly and unexpectedly losing her best friend of 21 years at the tender age of 32, and some of those closest to her doubting her purpose, just to name a few! Cynthia has survived, thrived, and become a warrior! More determined than ever, Cynthia has taken all that she has persevered through to teach other high-performing women how to be confident and victorious in every area of their life through the power of faith, prayer, and obedience to Christ, hence the title: "The Warfare Coach."

Academically, Cynthia has a Bachelor of Arts in Psychology, a Master's in Business Administration, a Juris Doctor, and is licensed to practice law in the State of Maryland. Professionally, Cynthia owns a growing law firm and works as a corporate attorney for a large national corporation. In ministry, she is a licensed minister and set to be ordained as an Elder while pursuing the path to becoming a pastor. Cynthia has helped to plant a church and a number of organizations/ministries over the years. In early 2019, Cynthia released her first book and is currently working on her second.

Cynthia enjoys singing the wrong lyrics loud and proud, vacationing at the beach, and spending time with her family. She lives by the mantra "If not now, when? If not you, who?" #noexcuses

BARBARA SULLIVAN

Dear Fear,

    I'll admit you won the first few rounds. You preyed on me from the start, working down from the generations before me, and I didn't stand a chance. I hate that you found such a comfortable place in my life. I hate that I listened to you for so long. I allowed you to bully me. Fear. I listened and let you surround me with people who only obliged you, those who only worked to keep me in your service. I let you whisper doubt in my ear, making me question everything I did. Fear, you lied about everything. You convinced me to pursue relationships and friendships that were not healthy, and sent your lackeys to lie to me as well. You knocked me down time and again, each time making me smaller and smaller. Your lies became detrimental to my mental and physical health. I'll even admit, Fear, that for a while there your lies kept me paralyzed. You prevented me from working toward God's plan for me, from working towards my dreams, from working on making myself happy.

    But guess what Fear? God made me smarter and stronger than you. I am fighting the good fight, and I've got my eye on the prize. I don't need you or your false comfort, Fear. I now know you and recognize you.

    You are the chains keeping me from my purpose. You tried to block my path and God used it as a detour to make me wiser, stronger, more determined. You are cunning Fear, a real smooth operator. That's what makes you my greatest teacher. God used everything you threw at me, everything you did to me, everything I allowed you to do – He used it for my story and HIS GLORY. I am the clay and He is my potter. God takes what you've given me and uses it to shape and mold me. Thank you, Fear. That sounds stupid to say, but I am so grateful to you. You, dearest Fear, provided the kiln to harden me, the pressure to turn me from a lump of coal into a diamond. God made me the strongest version of myself in my darkest hour and weakest place, and it was all because of you. But it is time for you to surrender or die Fear. God made me a fighter and you cornered me, so I'm coming out swinging. You may have won the battle but I will win the war. I will have the last word.

    Sincerely no longer yours,

    Barbara Taylor Sullivan

Dear Fear,
Thank you For Making Me Shine

Have you ever tried to change yourself by lowering your expectations, plastering on the smile, and looking or acting exactly like someone wants you to? Have you ever woken up one day and wondered when you became this version of yourself? You know, the version of you that is too depressed to face your high school reunion and every day feels like a panic attack waiting to happen? I have. I know that person all too well.

Let's sit down for a moment. Get comfortable, while I tell you my story. Let me tell you about how my life came together when it all fell apart. Let's talk about how I became unrecognizable to myself and those closest to me because I kept trying to fit into someone else's version of me. Let me tell you about...him.

I remember meeting him one day as a freshman in college. I wish I could tell a happy story where I met the most handsome and charming man that swept me off my feet, but that's not what happened. When I met him, there was something about him that told me to run. In about 3 minutes of meeting me, he was already talking about trying to get in my pants. I felt this energy that said that I should run because this would not end well. I walked away from that first meeting swearing I would never have anything to do with him. But he worked with my roommate and she kept telling me what a great guy he was. Maybe I was being too harsh? Maybe I misread that initial meeting? An opportunity presented itself where he was allowed a second meeting, and boy did he pounce on his chance.

Now that I've been through it I realize I should've just listened to my intuition and drowned the other voices out, but I didn't. I wasn't secure enough in my beliefs to stay true to myself. I want to scream at that young, stupid girl that thought "What's the worst that could happen?" I was stupid because I thought I was strong, but I was so very, very wrong. Once I let him in I fell and I fell hard. I fell for his stories and for the way he made me laugh. He seemed so genuinely invested in me, and all I had ever wanted was to be loved unconditionally by a husband that wanted to be my partner. I wanted someone who could be supportive of me with my strong opinions and big crazy dreams. I wanted someone who didn't want to change me. Was that too much to ask?

I thought this man was giving me everything I had ever wished for. I thought I could find wholeness in him. Now I know, that's where it all went wrong. I wasn't whole to start with, and I thought having someone to love me like that would be what I needed. He said and did all the right things, and it made me feel so good, at least in the beginning. I fell for the minimum effort he put into our relationship. At the time I didn't realize that I saw his minimum as all I deserved. That's that hindsight again. I just thought that we were both young and could figure it out. I thought that the more I could be like what he wanted, the more effort he would make. If I must be honest, here's the real truth - I fell for what I thought was all I deserved because I didn't realize how broken I was.

Don't get me wrong, I knew I had "issues" or things to work on. But the reality was, I was broken. There were potholes of insecurity left from my childhood. Insecurity because my mom had been divorced twice (gasp!), and my father wasn't consistently part of my life growing up. Insecurity from growing up in a single-parent household where we were doing good to get by. Lucky to pay the bills, have a roof over our heads and food to eat, but don't ask for anything else. The biggest insecurity being that I would never be able to have a healthy relationship because I had never actually witnessed one. Fear married my insecurities and I believed the people that told me I couldn't or wouldn't accomplish the big dreams that had been placed on my heart early in my life. Can you imagine as a child being told that I wouldn't succeed because I was female, and that my background and family situation would prevent me from achieving anything? The insecurities of having to change schools and make new friends constantly because we moved almost as much as a military family does. Because of this, I never felt like I fit in, and never felt like I belonged anywhere. Add in the insecurity from body image issues, oh I was a hot mess.

As I matured and came into adulthood, I thought I knew what holes were left, where they were, and that I had it all under control. I thought I could fake it until I made those holes disappear, that I could cover those insecurities with false confidence until it became real. I was feeling secure in myself, in who I was and where I was going to go in life. I had my plan and I met this guy that seemed to understand me, and fit into the plan. He seemed to fill whatever was left of those holes. What could possibly go wrong here?

As we continued to grow, it was time for the next step, marriage. I realized that, while I was comfortable "playing house", making a final commitment seemed too much. Why did I keep asking for confirmation that he was the man I was supposed to marry? If it was truly what God wanted for my life and a match made in heaven, then shouldn't I have peace and want the relationship to keep moving forward? Instead of taking God's silence on my questions as a no, I took his silence as confirmation to keep doing what I was doing. Surely if I were wrong HE would stop me, right? Nope, I needed to learn the lessons the hard way.

Fear kept me holding tight to this man, and kept me believing that I couldn't do any better. Fear told me to put a long timeline on the relationship, and I rationalized that we needed to make it through challenges so that we would overcome whatever would come in the future. Challenges only make you stronger as a couple, right? Now I know that I should've read those challenges as huge exit signs telling me to get out. God showed me who this man was, but I stayed. I stuck around thinking, "Surely, you're wrong God? I didn't hear you correctly." I don't have time to tell you about all the red flags in the relationship, and red flags about who I was in this relationship. Even back then I saw them, but fear kept telling me it was all okay.

Fear said to ignore the doubts from the jokes that fed my insecurities. Fear made me okay with the fact that he didn't like my friends, so I let them fall to the wayside. Did I look at it as giving up my friends? Of course not. My exact thought was something like, "Hey, I like his friends, so if we can hang out together with them then it's a win-win." I isolated myself and was clingy to the very thing that made me afraid. Fear led me to ignore the signs of deeper issues in him and myself. I thought we could rely on each other and be stronger together. I thought we were sharing each other's strengths. I didn't see that he was taking me down with him, drowning me as I was trying to save him. Fear had me standing by his side faithfully and blindly. It's been said that love is blind - I guess that phrase never made sense to me until this very moment. Love can be very, very blinding, especially when it's rooted in fear.

Fear works like kudzu. It takes over whatever is already there, covering it up and slowly killing what is underneath until all you see is a kudzu forest. Fear took root in me as a child and then grew to take over my relationships. Then it spilled over into the rest of my life until it was nothing but fear. I began to doubt my mission and purpose in life, something I had been sure about since I was 6 years old.

I struggled completing my Bachelor's Degree because I was focusing too much on my relationship and not enough on my studies. I was also working as much as possible to support myself, and sometimes him. I had this great job as an event photographer, so I never really complained about picking up extra hours or working events, until I realized what it was doing to my academic life. It was exhausting working that much for work and for school, and once I graduated with a history degree that I had no idea what I was going to do with, I felt completely lost. So again, I made a plan. I sought God's guidance of course, and a graduate degree seemed to be my next step. I continued on the academic path, much to the chagrin of my then fiancé, and I felt like I was back in my purpose. Fear caught my ear again and convinced me not to try for different opportunities during the program because it would mean having a long-distance relationship or spending too much time apart which would make my man unhappy. We all want to keep our men happy, right?

Fear paralyzed me after graduating with a master's degree. It just did not make sense to move my husband and new baby away from what we knew so that I could start a new career using my degree. Fear told me to listen when my husband thought I should go back to my photographer job, even after I left because I felt that season was finished. I listened to fear and returned, making the job into a full-time career because we needed the steady paycheck to support our family. Along every step of the path I gave fear, and this man, too much say over my life. I did it in my relationship, in my friendships, and in the direction of my life. I let fear win and allowed this flawed man, with his own insecurities, and fears, and holes in himself, to have that kind power and control over me. His fears fed my fears, and that fear continued to grow.

Did I know I was giving up my power? Of course not. It started in small things, and over years it just continued to add up until I became this smaller version of myself, quite literally there towards the end. Eventually my light dimmed so much I thought it had gone out. You may be wondering how I realized that I had given up so much of myself. Did I just wake up one morning and think, "Wow Barbara, you really need to get it together?" Or maybe, "My goodness, how is it that you are so smart but make such dumb decisions?" No, not really. It started with small realizations that just continued to add up until the problem could no longer be ignored. First was the thought that if you're happy then you should be at peace and fulfilled, right? But I realized that even though I could be happy with him and my life (momentarily anyway), I was so unhappy with myself and felt no peace about my life. When I would try to voice this feeling or try to make changes to correct my unhappiness, it became a source of contention between my husband and myself. How can me trying to better myself be something that makes him so angry? Why is it that the more I lean on God and try to build my faith, this man fights even harder against me? How can a man who says he loves me want to see me so unhappy? It was like every time I thought I was climbing out of the hole, he was there trying to push me further down. And because of fear, through all of these questions, I stayed and I fought.

I tried to change all of the things he didn't like, change all of the faults he pointed out. I tried to be less demanding, tried to be more "chill." I tried to be less "extra," and to be more whatever he wanted me to be. He thought my standards and expectations were too high and felt I needed to lower them. He would prey on my insecurities, saying that I just didn't understand how a relationship worked because I had never had a good example or that I didn't understand how men worked because my father had never been around to teach me. It was fear that kept me listening and believing him because there was an inkling of truth in it. Not much truth but enough to fertilize that seed of doubt already in me.

Each time I tried to change myself and be what he wanted, I got weaker and died a little more inside. I literally feel like I turned myself inside out, upside down, and every which way I could to try to make him happy. Here's the thing though, I wasn't happy because I didn't feel like I could be myself. It seemed like nothing I did could make him happy. I felt like a failure – in my marriage and life. I was depressed. I felt burnt out. I lived my life anxiously; walking on eggshells all the time afraid of what would be the next thing to set my husband off and cause a blowup, or my boss for that matter who had a similar temperament. To say the least, I was stressed and it took a major toll on my body. I felt like my body was attacking itself, probably because the stress was causing my body to attack itself. My husband and I both became angry ALL THE TIME. I felt worthless because my marriage was failing. I felt miserable because I was not where I wanted to be in life. I began to think that I was only good at helping others succeed but not myself. I felt under-appreciated for the value I brought, at home and work. So what did I do? I stayed, hoped, and prayed.

Then the first major blow came. He chose "out". "I love you as the mother of my children, but I am not in love with you anymore," he said. Can you imagine how that felt? This man I had given everything to and had changed so much of myself for – he no longer loved me. It wasn't something said in the heat of the moment, out of anger, or in some attempt to hurt me. I could see it on his face, but I just thought I should keep trying to make it work. I wanted it to work for the sake of our children because I was sure he didn't mean it. I wanted it to work because marriage is supposed to be forever, not something you just quit. I wanted to keep my promise to God and our families. Honestly, I wanted it to work because I didn't want to be a failure and I couldn't admit defeat.

It was time for different tactics. Instead of sticking with my usual relationship with God, a relationship where I only went to Him when things were good or when I had a request, I began to seek God's guidance in everything. I would attend bible study in the morning and at night. I began praying for the Lord to lead my path. I prayed harder and rejoiced for all of the challenges I was facing. Full disclosure though, it was not completely sincere. My prayers were selfish because I believed that these prayers would somehow make God save my marriage. I was still coming from a place of what I wanted, and I was still trying to manipulate the outcome to be what I thought was best for me. There's me being a control freak, trying to tell God what His plan for me is. I tried daily to be more grateful and to change my mentality. I worked on myself and my attitude. And somehow, the fights became more frequent and more intense.

Eventually, I became weary of the fight. Life is too short to live that way. I asked God again to lead my path. I asked for Him to remove from my life what wasn't from Him or for Him. If God didn't put it there then I didn't want it. Funny enough, not long after that prayer my husband said those words again. In the middle of a prayer where I was trying to thank God for this man and everything he does for our family, I was accused of not caring about or loving my husband. He stated again that he was no longer in love with me, followed by he wanted a divorce. I was completely shattered inside but the tears stopped when he said this. I heard God tell me to stop fighting, to stop resisting. I let the pain of what my husband was telling me to sink in, and instead of tears, the pain made me realize that I felt the same way. I was no longer in love with him.

Not only that, but I realized in that moment that I never should've let the relationship get this far. God had allowed it to continue and reach this point to teach me a lesson. I could see how much I had been broken down by this relationship and the compromises I had made in myself. I hold on to things much longer than I should, and not everything is meant to last a lifetime. After admitting these truths to myself, I oddly felt peace. Once again, I heard Him say "Stop resisting," and I realized that this is what God had been telling me for so long and I was too scared and stubborn to admit to myself. Somewhere in the thirteen years we had spent together my husband and I had gotten to a place where neither one of us liked, let alone loved, one another. We only saw each other as enemies now, always on the defense waiting for an attack. I don't know much, but I know that's not how a marriage should work. I finally got it. I finally heard what God was saying, and I understood that I was not meant to continue fighting this fight. I was ready to step out of the ring and hang up my gloves.

I finally admitted out loud he was right, I didn't love him anymore. Once I let that truth out, everything else I had been holding in came with it. The fact that I felt that our marriage was tearing me apart, that it had become detrimental to me emotionally, mentally, and physically. The fact that I felt like I had to pretend to be someone I wasn't to try to make him happy and that left me feeling like a hollow shell. All of these things were not entirely his fault, I played my part in it all. I made the decision to change myself to suit him. I let the fear and the fighting make me a different person. We agreed that divorce was the best option for us, but since Christmas was a week away we would wait until after the holidays to change anything or let anyone know.

At this point, I went into self-preservation mode. I started putting myself and my children first, and not factoring him into the equation. I wanted to get back to me and follow my dreams and passions. I wanted to go where God called me. About this time, I also decided that I would run for the open U.S. Senate seat for Alabama as an Independent Candidate. Yes, seriously. Because my life wasn't enough of a mess, I thought I'd add some more to the mix. I've felt that public office was always my calling from a young age. Even when I would try to pursue another avenue or thought that maybe I was being selfish for wanting that, God would find a way to bring me back and stir up those passions again. I thought now was my chance. Perfect timing since the seat was open, and the bonus that now I didn't have to listen to someone else's opinion about when it would be acceptable, how I should go about it, what beliefs I could and could not promote on my platform.

We continued to live together through the holidays, and it was ROUGH. I tried to continue to be normal around my now estranged husband, but how can you be "normal" around someone who no longer loves you? How can you be "normal" when someone does not support what you are trying to do to build yourself back up? There was no merry Christmas in our house, in fact, everyone in the house came down with the flu for Christmas. The only thing happy about the New Year was the prospect that it was a new year and a new beginning. Now that I was going to need to support myself and our children at least fifty percent of the time, I would need to find a new job that would hopefully mean less stress, better pay, and fewer hours away from home. The new year seemed like the perfect time to make all of these changes to help turn my life around and to get rid of everything that had been causing me anxiety and misery for so long. When I told my husband about this plan it only angered him. He couldn't understand how I could leave a "good" job without having another job lined up. Since we were still living together and splitting bills, I allowed myself to listen to that fear he was feeding in me and I stayed at the job I hated.

I listened to the fear that I wasn't ready to move out on my own yet.

I hadn't yet realized that it was fear holding me back. I continued to trust that this man still had my best interest at heart. Pretty foolish of me, huh? Once again, I was in that pressure cooker, literally dreading waking up every single day. I lived each day on edge, just praying to make it through to the end. I was constantly sick because all of that anxiety was wreaking havoc on my nervous and immune systems, literally becoming a smaller version of myself. I was losing weight no matter what I did. As someone who is very petite to start with, losing weight is not a good thing, in fact, it's downright scary. This wasn't living, this was barely existing.

Finally, after a major panic attack because of the stress from work and my marriage, I decided the only way out of this mess was to start changing my situation no matter what. I took a week off of work to rest because I needed it, and used the time to apply for new jobs. I had to return to work after that week, but I had gotten the process started. Within a week I was called for an interview for one of the positions I applied for and ended up getting the job. I thought it was all coming together, that my prayers were finally being answered. I was still living with a husband who didn't love me but he also had not filed for divorce yet. We were coexisting with each other when necessary for the sake of the kids. Very unconvincingly I might add. This new job seemed like it was a start in the right direction for me. My husband and I discussed how I would start the new job and we would file for divorce once I was established in the job and my new place and we could afford a divorce. I started to make plans and look forward to what my life would look like in the future.

There's an old Yiddish proverb that says, "We plan, God laughs." Let me tell you God has laughed at almost every single one of my plans I've had over the last four years, at least. I think He may have laughed hardest when I began to invest in this new job and make plans for my new life. I started my new job at the beginning of March 2020 - smack dab in the middle of a global pandemic. Twelve days later, the office manager called me into her office to let me know I was being let go because of COVID-19 health precautions and the economic impact that a pandemic might bring. I worked a job that I thought was the answer to my prayers for less than two weeks before God laughed and said, "Yeah…. no. Just kidding."

Once again, all of my plans for my life failed and fell apart. Once again, I was left with nothing, feeling lost, and not knowing what to do or where to go. Strangely, I was not as panicked as I would have been previously, in fact, I felt very much at peace. I had spent so much time over the last few months praying and relying on God's grace and guidance, that I knew He would see me through this storm. But this peace I found, and my calm during the storm, only drove my estranged husband even crazier and he became very volatile. I was told my decisions were irrational and I was acting out of my norm. I was told that everything I was trying to do during this time would be more things that I started but never finished. Let me just say that I finish EVERYTHING I start, to the point of holding on to things far longer than I should because of the time invested. Then I was told nearly every day to get out of the house we shared and that I still paid bills for. While all of us will have tribulation and suffering, we are not supposed to live our lives being miserable – especially not in marriage. Here we are at the end of March and my estranged husband still hadn't done anything towards filing a divorce, but wanted to wage mental and emotional warfare on me daily. I no longer had on my gloves and no longer wanted in that ring, but it didn't stop him from trying to goad me back into the fight.

All I can say is, but God. I later found out that COVID-19 had found its way through the office I had been working at and God protected me and my family through my unemployment during this time. I was able to claim unemployment because of the government shutdown, so I was still getting paid and able to support myself and the kids. Those unemployment benefits also allowed me to be able to file for divorce because that process still hadn't been started 4 months after we made that decision. I was able to use the time I was unemployed focusing on myself and on getting closer to God. I had already lost everything and felt so broken that I would die, and yet I lived. I realized I needed to let go of that fear that had been holding on for so long. I began weeding it out of my life and my soul. Relying on God forced me to pay closer attention to the things and people He placed in front of me. It allowed me to be more discerning about my path and where I spent my energies. Now was my time.

Honestly, 2019 was not a good year for me, and 2020 has not been a great year for anyone. All it took was a divorce, a job change, a job loss, a global pandemic, and moving back in with my mom for me to decide to kick the habit of fear. At this point, what else can I lose? Now I can see that it was all part of God's plan. I may not be able to see the big picture or know how the story ends, but I can see that everything leading up to this point was honestly for the best. That pressure cooker that tried to destroy me made me stronger, like the pressure needed to turn coal into a diamond. The divorce forced my ex-husband and I to deal with underlying issues that we both kept trying to sweep under the rug, which only caused our relationship to deteriorate. Now that we're divorced, my ex-husband has to engage with the kids and be involved to have a relationship with them. The warfare in my marriage forced me to finally stand up for myself and stop letting others take advantage or walk all over me, in all aspects of my life. I better understand boundaries and the necessity of saying no.

After the initial pain, my ex-husband felt from the divorce and my move with the kids, and after he lashed out at me because of that pain, we finally got to a place of amicability. We can speak to each other like friends again, something we haven't been able to do with each other for years. We can be honest with each other without any expectations or being defensive. The divorce has also helped us to get on the same page with parenting, for the most part anyway. We couldn't be a united team while we were married, but somehow the divorce has allowed us to make that happen. Maybe it forced us to make it happen, but either way, I'm happy with the results. Because of my forced time at home, I've been able to spend more time with my kids and working on myself. I've been able to walk with my kids through the changes going on in our family, as well as the changes they had to experience when their lives were turned upside down because of COVID-19.

I've probably done more for myself, and my children, regarding physical and mental health in the last 6 months than I have in the last 4 years.

I couldn't have done any of this without God. It took God literally putting my back against a wall and making my world fall apart for me to finally stop questioning if I was hearing him correctly, stop resisting, and learn to trust in Him and Him alone. I know it sounds crazy to say that God wanted me to divorce my husband, but I believe that to be true. That's what God was showing me, but I kept questioning if I heard Him correctly. Once I obeyed and stopped fighting, I had so many confirmations that this was exactly what was supposed to happen. Staying together for the sake of your children is well-intentioned, it's not always the best option. Your kids know when you're unhappy. They're not oblivious to tension, aggression, or arguments between their parents, even when you think you're doing a good job of hiding it from them. They know - they're observant, they see all, they hear all, and they feel all. My kids can now grow up seeing that even though their parents couldn't stay married, we still love them and it had nothing to do with them. I hope that this approach may help to keep our children from being as broken and consumed with fear as I was. Hopefully, the fear kudzu will not take over their lives. Maybe they won't have to learn these lessons the hard way because they won't have those same fears and insecurities.

That's my hope, but I won't make any plans for it. I'll just pray about it, along with everything else, and leave it in God's hands.

Who are you living your life for? Are you living to please others, please yourself, or please God? Are you letting your relationships rule you? (Your answer to those questions can help you find the change you need to make to overcome what is blocking you from your next.)

_____

_____

_____

_____

Are you managing your fear, or is fear managing you? What are 2 small steps you can build upon to take back your life and beat back the fear that is taking over?

_____

_____

_____

_____

Bio:

Barbara Sullivan was born in California and spent most of her childhood in Missouri before moving to Alabama in middle school. After graduating from Northview High School in Dothan, Alabama, Barbara went on to receive a Bachelors of Arts degree in History from Auburn University and a Masters of Public Administration from Auburn University Montgomery. She currently lives in Auburn, Alabama with her two sons, Sebastian and Eli.

Barbara has a varied background. She pursued several different majors in different subject areas at Auburn before deciding on history, and she worked as a professional event photographer for over 12 years. Barbara's love for history, government, and politics lead to a teaching position for middle school social studies in Montgomery. She also coaches her school's scholars bowl team.

While many of her interests are academic, Barbara also enjoys being outdoors. On weekends, you may find her hiking, swimming, or golfing. She also enjoys traveling and getting to explore new places, especially meeting new people and learning about different cultures. When she is at home Barbara enjoys baking and reading, as well as artistic pursuits like writing and painting.

Barbara is most passionate about God, her family, history and government. These are what fuel her and drive her forward in her journey. Knowing she is human and flawed, Barbara understands she is perfectly imperfect and has to continuously ask for God's grace and mercy. It is HIS grace and mercy that have kept her alive and helped her to overcome. Because of this, she also knows the importance of allowing herself and others grace because no one is perfect and we all make mistakes. She strives to continuously spread kindness and love to others, hoping to shine a little light in the darkness having known firsthand the struggles that we all try to hide.

"Darkness cannot drive out darkness, only light can do that. Hate cannot drive out hate, only love can do that." – Dr. Martin Luther King, Jr.

JACKEY JACKSON

Dear Fear,

You can no longer have my purpose. This bastard child that has always seemed to struggle with finding her place in life is no longer distracted by you. Fear you have used me against me long enough and have worked in my life as a noisy pestilence way too long. They say the most valuable piece of property is the space between your ears and with great pleasure, fear, I serve you your eviction notice. All of your belongings: doubt, insecurities, loneliness, low self-esteem, and unworthiness have been destroyed, locks have been changed and you are being advised to stay away.

While you have taken residence, my life has been miserable. With you, fear, I felt depressed and lost. The worst part of all was realizing how much of my life I missed out on because I was not living in the moment, for that moment. I was not living on purpose. Fear you used the noisy pestilence to speak overtime and cause so much chaos in my mind. So much that I became totally distracted from the purpose that God chose for me. Looking back, I see how you strategically caused me to be derailed from my purpose by paralyzing me with doubt, always wondering "what if" or "why not". When it was not doubt or confusion you used insecurities. I swear it seemed like I never fit in anywhere. When doubt or insecurities were not top of mind and I thought I had obtained some footage you would find a way to make me feel so unworthy and leave me waddling in low self-esteem. Fear, you have caused me to self-sabotage and hold myself back from living daily in my purpose fearlessly, but I refuse to be captive any longer.

Fearless and Worthy,

Jackey Jackson

Dear Fear, You Can't Have My Purpose

Why am I here? Besides being a mother, wife, daughter, aunt, niece, cousin, friend, and colleague, what is my assignment here on earth? What is my purpose? What is my identity tied to? Why am I REALLY here? For many years of my life those questions have plagued me. While I was grateful for the purpose that God created me for, I realized that not functioning in your purpose was worse than not knowing it. How do I know? Been there, done that, and I have the t-shirt, mug, and emotional bondage to match.

Imagine having a cough, runny nose, headache then body ache, thinking you have a bad cold. Later you find out, you don't just have a cold but walking pneumonia and you are just knocked off your feet and restricted from everything. That's how fear works. Fear will disguise itself in the symptoms of other things. It was not always the feeling of being afraid, but in my life it showed up as procrastination, people-pleasing, sickness in my body, emotions all over the place at times, feeling like a victim and not knowing who to trust. What is so disheartening for me is that I wanted to live that purpose-filled life that I had heard about. I wanted to witness the fearless life I believed to have witnessed in the lives of others. However, too often I felt unworthy and not good enough to take the first step to pursue my purpose.

The first step. It's always the first step. I realized it wasn't ONE thing that halted my movement, but a plethora of things that either happened or didn't happen that stopped me from moving forward. It's hard to take a step when you are paralyzed from fear. I was stuck. I felt stuck, stuck in my emotions, stuck in my ability to move, and stuck in a lack of confidence. I felt like I lost my ability to speak and represent myself freely. If you add in the thoughts that I believed everyone thought of me, now I was stuck and tormented. Can you relate? Have you ever felt paralyzed and unmoving in your purpose? Have you ever questioned yourself because of what others may think? If so, I get it. I want to tell you that you do have a choice. Right now, on today, take a moment to choose destiny over defeat, and success over stuck!

Let's continue on this journey. I've always considered myself an introvert and because of this and life encounters, I used it as a cop-out to not speak freely. I love people, I serve people, and enjoy having a good time with people but somewhere along the line, my voice was silenced. I never sought to find my voice, or fight for my voice. I wouldn't have known where to start.

My first encounter with my voice being silenced was as a child. See my dad was a hard working guy, he worked two full-time jobs and several part-time hustles and my mom was a nurse. I was that latchkey kid growing up with a strong father who believed children stayed in their place and you followed the instructions given. I don't recall **conversations** with my parents but **instructions** from my parents. I grew up before the cell phone age so whatever the plan was the night before was it, and your instructions were left on the refrigerator. So when I became pregnant in high school, telling my parents was not an easy task. I felt alone as a child with not many people to communicate with. The search for friends in high school led to a pregnancy that continued to fuel my spirit of rejection. Derailed, scared, and alone, those are all the emotions to express how I felt when the father of my child wanted nothing to do with this pregnancy. Add in the reaction of my father who didn't want me to keep the baby and forbade my mother to help me, I was heartbroken. As a parent now, I understand that my dad was doing the best he knew how, and only wanted to ensure I didn't miss out on any opportunities. I just wish he would have communicated that with love. I needed love.

I escaped my dad's disappointment and became a wife to someone I barely knew. In only a few years, I found myself divorced and rejected all over again. "There must be something wrong with me", I thought. I didn't have much time to sit in despair, as I had a child to consider. Like many mothers, I put my healing on the back burner so that I could be functional for my child.

Functioning came in the form of working hard. That was one thing I was good at. I finished high school and was determined to not be another statistic. I always felt like I had to work harder because my dad would remind me that I was up against either more seasoned colleagues or those that had gone on to college and had more education than I. Was that true? Maybe. But because my dad left out the encouragement, all I heard was "You'll never be good enough". Derailed again. Voice silenced. Rejection digging deeper. This was all before the age of 20.

My hard work eventually paid off and at 22 I was able to purchase my first home for me and my son. At 22 with your own home, you can find many friends, especially those who still live at home and want a place to go to do all the things they can't do at home. When you don't understand boundaries you let anyone in your personal space. Living in my rejection, I allowed too many people to have access to me that never should have. Once I was used up and no longer beneficial to their lives, I was left to pick up the pieces alone. Fear convinced me I needed them. I didn't need them, I needed to heal.

I wish then that I understood better about discernment, boundaries, affirmations, balance, and self-care. I wish I was taught this as a child. I understand that life happens, however being able to discern the distractions of life attempting to keep you out of the will of God is essential. Anytime you step out of the will of God it will cause a derailment. It's important on your journey that you know how to categorize the people in your life. It doesn't matter if it's mentors (everyone is not your mentor, some people are persons you admire), mentee, listening ear, trusted advisor, coach, friend, enemy, road dog, etc and use the appropriate boundary. I neglected my self care because I didn't set boundaries. I wasted my talents in pivotal seasons of my life because I was consumed with pleasing people. When the day came for me to be deprogrammed and learn new behaviors and how to set boundaries, I struggled.

Discouraged, because of too many setbacks I started to doubt and question my own existence. Fear reminded me of the little girl that felt unworthy, rejected and derailed. I was a mess, a hot one. Even in my mess, I found my way back to Jesus. He saved ME, the hot mess, unworthy, rejected, lost daughter. I realized that I missed my relationship with God, and how to effectively communicate with Him. I realized then that communication or a lack of communication has been the worst for me. The lack of communication in most of my decisions and/or relationships have been the pits. I struggled to communicate effectively with people I could SEE, which means

I absolutely struggled to communicate with God. See I found myself afraid to talk to God because he could have been disappointed in me as well. There was a chance that at some point He may leave me also. I allowed my rejection to dictate my surrendering. Hearing a Pastor speak on how our relationship especially communication with our earthly father has a great deal as to how we respond/connect to our Heavenly Father really hit home for me. It was probably the first time that I was able to self examine my relationship with God as to how we communicate. Nobody likes anyone who only speaks to them when they are asking for something or just repeating the same thing over and over when they do decide to check in.

After a lot of derailments, I eventually realized that God has been the only common denominator in my life. When I found myself alone when I found myself afraid or confused he was the only name that I could call on to find some solace. If I could find the strength to stay in his presence long enough, I discovered I had enough strength to get back up. But even here at this junction, the struggle is real. Coincidentally just like there were several derailments along the way, there have been several alignments that positioned me back into purpose. I became an entrepreneur, and that changed my world. Here is where I learned some valuable lessons and principles on personal growth, mindset, and affirmations. After years of not achieving and self-sabotaging myself I understood that I had to dig deep and get to the root of the thing(s) that are/were hindering me. I had to face some things, speak to some things, change from some things, and leave from some things. I knew that until those things were addressed and addressed properly it would always be there waiting for the most inconvenient time to show up and bring about a setback. You can only take a pain pill for pain but so long. Eventually, you become immune but if you can identify the source and correct that which brings the pain you can begin the process of living pain free. Knowing your triggers is so important so that you can daily stay on track. I know now that to experience the fullness that God intended, I have to trust God more and silence the voices that did not speak God's language, and protect my space. To be effective I would have to unsilence myself and not be afraid to speak in the rooms and at the tables, I would be afforded to share at.

When I began to write this chapter, there were times when I would feel confused about sharing, but I continued to trust God. I understand that I am to "Seek Ye First". Even if I'm confused about the next step, I know that if I seek God first, and trust him with my life, then everything will always work out for my good, and most importantly the purpose he ordained will be fulfilled on the earth. I struggled way too long. It was beyond time that I got my voice back, and no longer will I allow fear to rob me of who I am. I am no longer paralyzed. I am more than worthy. I am walking in confidence. I am living my purpose-filled life, and God will forever get the glory.

So why are you here and not yet living your best purpose-filled life? Get unstuck, shake the very thing off of you that is holding you back. Understand that we crawl until we can stand tall and walk. You didn't get in the mess overnight, and you won't get out of it overnight, but you must start somewhere. And if you have been the cause of derailment for someone else, repent. You were not put here on the earth to derail others but to plant or water seeds that God's love and beauty could be reproduced in the earth.

Here are a few things I want to leave with you that's helped me on my journey.

Hebrews 13:6 (ESV) So we can confidently say, "The Lord is my helper; I will not fear; what can man do to me? What if we read that again and stop at fear. So we can confidently say, "The Lord is my helper; I will not fear. Let's read it again and replace fear with the feeling or hindrance you are feeling. So we can confidently say, "The Lord is my helper; I will not procrastinate. So we can confidently say, "The Lord is my helper; I will not fear communicating effectively. Whatever emotion we experience that is not of God we have to remember that we have a helper to help us through.

What would be your replacement word? Rewrite the above, so that it speaks to your situation.

_____

_____

1 John 4:18 There is no fear in love. But perfect love drives out fear. I will also encourage you if you are feeling fearful to the point of paralyzation and confusion, check your love tank. Too often we can be surrounded by people yet feel lonely. The feeling of loneliness brings on the feeling of not being loved. While we are looking to be loved there is great possibility that there is one direction you neglected to turn to for love and that was toward your Heavenly Father. Now you may not get a card in the mail, but God will send you a message to your heart. He will show you he cares when he gives you a strategy to get the project complete without procrastination. He will show you He cares when writing the paper becomes easy. God loves us more than we know and his love helps to remove the fears. His help allows you to set the boundaries and not fear the opinion of others. See I had to realize that God has a vested interest in me. He loves me and cares for me because not only did he give me a purpose but he committed to helping me succeed in my purpose. It's all for me to live a fulfilled (good) life and a life that glorifies the Father.

Is your "love tank" low? What can you do to help refuel your love tank through Christ Jesus?

_____

_____

Dear Fear You can NOT have my PURPOSE.

I serve you your eviction notice. All of your belongings: doubt, insecurities, loneliness, low self-esteem, and unworthiness have been destroyed, locks have been changed and you are being advised to stay away.

Bio:

Jacqueline "Jackey" Jackson is a native Washingtonian who currently resides in Upper Marlboro, MD. Jackey is married and the mother of two sons and one daughter and loves any time spent with family especially her 93 year old mom. After three layoffs within two years, in 2015 Jackey stepped out on faith to take the road of entrepreneurship becoming a full time Realtor. Remembering her own personal experience of becoming a first time homeowner at the age of 22, followed by loads of debt and years of financial rebuilding to purchase again, Jackey's passion is to help others build wealth through real estate not just sale or purchase a home.

In 2019 KeyXchange LLC was formed out of passion to extend beyond real estate and be able to help educate, coach and give back to the community because her desire is to help my community learn to obtain wealth, grow wealth and then share wealth. Jackey is excited about the launch of "Business Women Building", a community for women to come together to listen, learn and leverage best practices to grow their business, while being in an environment to connect, confide and celebrate each other. Her ultimate goal is to help others successfully navigate through their own personal transformation to obtain the necessary breakthrough, to live freely and joyfully while on their purpose filled journey of life.

CIERRA AVERY

Dear Fear,

I gave you too much access and you've controlled me in more ways than one. You engulfed me in doubt which led to shame. You made me feel unworthy, lonely, angry, sad, guilty, doubtful but most of all depressed. You consumed me so much until I became unrecognizable even to myself. I took comfort in low self-esteem because my life reflected that I didn't deserve any more than what I had already possessed (which was a little to nothing). I began to allow others to hurt me and abuse me (verbally and physically). I allowed others to break me in places that I didn't realize had any room left to be broken. I was at a point in life where all I knew was pain and anxiety. Fear you made me feel the only way I'd escape you was to plan my death and I mean plan it in a way that it looked like an accident. I was so confused and conflicted about feeling this way because all my life people had been telling me Cierra you're different and God has a call on the inside of you. I was supposed to know that I was born with greatness on the inside of me but all I felt was you (FEAR) and all of the lies that you had filled me with. From the time I was born you told me that I wasn't enough, no one will ever truly love you, you are worthless. You told me God couldn't use me and that I would never be who God said I was. You tried to own me.

You messed up when I lost it ALL. I lost my job, my car, the few healthy relationships that I did have and almost lost my mind. I mean you stripped me down to nothing but nothing pushed me into something. God began to speak to me and reminded me of Isaiah 55:11 and reversed everything that you said about me. I found that I am more than enough, he loves me unconditionally and I'm worth more than anything money can buy to him. Not only did he predestined me, He called me, He Justified me and he's getting ready to glorify me because I turned my mess into a YES!

So now I raise a standard against you, fear, with the Lord of hosts as my army and I will be the beginning of the break in the generational curses that have had my family trapped and bound for years. Because I found me in him, I am declaring freedom for me and everything connected to me. Thank you fear for pushing me into God's plans and promise for my life. I know you didn't plan for it to end this way but in the back of my mind, I knew that the God I served always had the final say! So, fear my final words to you are Access DENIED!

Signed,

Cierra Avery

Dear Fear, I Survived it!

It took me a while to write this because there is so much that I have to say. There is so much that I was afraid to speak about out of concern and fear of how I'd make others feel. The reality is, God spoke and I must obey! We have to stop allowing the fear of what we see and feel makes us miss what God has said concerning our seasons of YES. A "YES" season is that season of growth and elevation that may be uncomfortable, lonely, painful, exposing, and unfamiliar, but necessary for your elevation. While there are still areas in my life that God is revealing and healing, I did not want to miss the opportunity to share with you how he saved me. I didn't want to miss out on a moment to share how I learned to gather my broken pieces, lay them at the feet of Jesus, and THRIVE because I survived. My prayer is that you can see the triumph over the obstacles that the enemy used to kill me, but God used to strengthen me.

It was 1990, the year of the millennials, and the beginning of a new era. To many, life was simple and free. Then there was me, being born to a mother, absent father, and straight into bondage with depression and death attached at the hip. The enemy wasted absolutely no time speaking negative things over me and trying to take me out. It started when I was just an infant. As a kid, I was reminded often of the story of my birth. It was the typical story of a woman giving birth. My mom allowed a family member in the room with her as I was being born, she pushed, pushed and pushed and out came this baby. Where most people would say this was the most beautiful moment for my mother. This story doesn't end like that. As the story goes, my mother had a baby that was so ugly that the family member ran out of the delivery room screaming "what is that! that baby is ugly!". This led to being nicknamed "Ugly Ugly" which stuck with me for the majority of my life.

When the story was told, I laughed, because everyone else thought it was funny. I didn't want to display pain or defeat in what they found humorous. I went along to get along. Little did they know, their laughs planted a seed in me that I was undesirable ugly and unwanted. This kicked off my low self-esteem and issues of beauty, long before I knew the definitions of such.

When I was about 5 years old at White oak park down on highway 95 in Eufaula Al, I had a face to face moment with fear that I can never forget. I was there along with my mom and 4 older siblings walking in a straight line from oldest to youngest alongside the edge of the lake. Because none of us knew how to swim, the only way we were allowed to touch the water was if we walked along the side of it. For some reason me just touching the surface of the water was not good enough for the enemy. Somehow, I ended up underwater and my body had drifted mid-lake before anyone realized I was no longer in formation. My mom and sisters began to call and look for me but got no answer. My mother began to panic and my sisters began to cry. I remember hearing my mother yell for the only person she knew could help, she began to call on the name of Jesus. Within seconds my body shot up out of the water and a nearby swimmer gathered my limp body out of the water and my mom performed CPR to revive me. It was in that moment that my life changed.

As I recovered, I had no recollection of what happened. My mother continued to wail "the devil tried to take my baby from me!". I was already a target before grade school. At an early age, I not only witnessed but experienced several strongholds and curses that had attached themselves to my family lineage years before I was born. What my family suppressed, the enemy exposed. The "don't look like what you're going through mentality" was taking my family out, and they had no idea. My family was taught to MASK in public and bleed in private. But then, there was me. I bled everywhere. I wore what I felt and I wore it well. It didn't matter the emotion; shame, doubt, anger, guilt, sadness, I wore it all. I allowed each of these things to consume me so much until I was unrecognizable to myself. There was nothing but pain around me so I took comfort in every emotion that I was faced with because life taught me that I didn't deserve any better. To make matters worse, all of my siblings were special to someone. There were all somebody's "baby" except lil old "ugly ugly". All I had was my mom who was always working to provide. She was never around much, and because of this I always felt tolerated over desired. I was always the one to understand my mother the most. I heard the late night cries, and I saw the tears. While our story isn't perfect, she is indeed one of the most amazing moms you could ask for.

Trials were an understatement and pain was the only statement we knew. The abuse became a major factor in our lives. I never felt an ounce of hatred towards my mom, because I knew her actions were not based on how much she loved me, but how little she felt loved. Being abused led me to start searching and accepting whatever I could get. Fear whispered in my ear that I didn't deserve more and that better was not my portion. I began to allow others to hurt and abuse me (verbally, mentally, and physically) because that was the language of love that had been shown and expressed to me my entire life. That was the love I knew.

I willingly gave others permission and power to break me in places that I didn't realize had room left to be broken. I had gotten so comfortable in the pain that I went from being the victim to the antagonizer. There has not been one relationship that I've ever entered into that I didn't leave without being talked down to, beat on, and broken-hearted. Want to know the shocking part? It was never by men, but by women figures, I had placed in my life to fill voids of not having a father or an active mom. I began to initiate the cycles of violence because it was the only way I knew how to receive the love that I knew to be real. I felt that if you were not hitting me to say you loved me, then I was unnecessary to you. Ironically, I started doing things to provoke and produce the environment that I was used to yet I was so desperate to get away from. That was the lowest part of my life. Low self-esteem had taken over. I was a walking suicide bomb. I was beyond angry, tired, sad, depressed, hurt, and broken. I began attempting to hurt myself by erasing my skin, cutting myself, and hiding it very well. I needed help. I'm so grateful that God never leaves the righteous forsaken. He sent me help right during my death.

In 2001 my godmother entered into my life and she entered with a charge. I was rough around the edges but she saw beyond that. She showed me that love had no limits but contained boundaries. I learned that I could be disciplined without being abused. I was her assignment. She didn't back down or run from it. She saw the task, the mess, the brokenness, and still agreed. Her "YES" activated my "WHY". I began to understand more that I was here for a purpose and God's love for me.

In 2019, I fell into a deep depression that God had to reach in and save me. I had given yet another human permission to "love" me the wrong way. I fell into such a dark space that I couldn't get out of bed to save my life. I couldn't sleep and my thoughts were no longer my own. I went from doctor to doctor from hospital to hospital and all they knew and no one had an answer. I was dropping weight so quickly, it was unhealthy. My blood levels and oxygen were low, and I had stopped eating. The thought of death became my very best friend. I stopped reaching out and responding to people, I called in for days at a time from work and I made it my business to make sure God knew I was angry with him. Why? I felt as if God allowed me to go through the cycles of pain instead of helping me. He was supposed to guide me..right? Protect me...right? Then why did I feel so alone and discarded? Fear kept me in that place. I was afraid to come out of that place because no one would be waiting for me on the other side. On September 2019, I gathered up any painkillers that I could find, and googled "how many of these 50 ml can I take to overdose?" I remember it like it was yesterday. I had 4 different piles of medication 20 pain pills in one pile 10 pain pills in the other fresh prescription of 30 sleeping pills and a brand new bottle of Excedrin I was content and comfortable with my decision to end this miserable thing that I called life and I was ok to end It with no goodbyes.

BUT GOD

How many know that there is and will always be a BUT God? God began to show me that He brought me to my absolute lowest to truly do a reset in me and to show me that my going "through" would not be in vain. He brought me to a place where

I had two options...suicide or submission. Conviction settled in. I put the pills down. The sleepless nights continued, but this time it was different. I was no longer alone but in conversation with God. During those sleepless nights, I began to hear God clearer than I ever had in my life. God spoke to me and told me "the people had to leave you because you HAD placed them before ME, they had to hurt you because you expected them to heal you, you felt discarded because that void was not made to be filled by man, GIVE ME MY seat back in your life! The Time is NOW!" I had no understanding of what it meant, but now I do. God began to replay my life before my eyes while showing me one of the many ministries that would be birthed out of what I thought was purposeless pain... the ISURVIVED IT ministry. This ministry helps others identify, rectify, and stop justifying the things that were temporarily sent. It helps others discover the strengths that we decided to harbor as weaknesses.

I learned that being submissive to God was more than a cliche but a blessing bigger than I imagined. All of those things that I viewed as faults God did a 360 with them He showed me that even the broken parts of me are beautiful. I learned that sometimes to Heal you have to go back to the thing that broke you. When you go back, you don't go alone. You go back with the Lord of hosts fighting with and for you/ God showed me that total restoration wouldn't take place until I learned that suppressing was not a form of healing. We have got to stop allowing what we feel, make us doubt what God said. It's called robbery by fear. For God's will to manifest, we have to DIE. Our old mindsets and gods we created have to DIE. Anything that isn't of our Father will have to bow to his will. This is the season for you to regain your strength and nutrients. Your strength comes from reading the word of God DAILY and communing with Him. Your nutrients come from building a strong and HEALTHY prayer life that will sustain your strength.

A true child of the champion knows that pain produces purpose. If I survived then so can you. Just put your trust in God and know that everything that you are faced with is predestined for you so walk Tall, Walk Heavy, and stay Ready with the Whole Armor of God.

Are you currently in an unhappy, unhealthy, or dysfunctional relationship (romantic or platonic) that you are scared of getting out of? Go deep and evaluate what you are afraid of and what that fear is based in.

_____

_____

_____

_____

Think about the narrative you often tell yourself when experiencing your fears. What truths can be said to combat those lies?

_____

_____

_____

_____

Bio:

Cierra L. Avery, the native of Eufaula, Alabama, is a speaker, coach, author, and CEO. She is the baby of five girls and was raised by a God-fearing single mom. At an early age, Cierra experienced domestic violence which lasted through adulthood, and battled with depression, anxiety, and rejection. Throughout life, she's fought to love all of her while trying to survive a life of domestic violence. It wasn't until Cierra was unexpectedly placed in ministry that she had to face her fears head on, only to discover her God-given purpose and passion to help others survive and teach them how to live a life of thriving!

For years, Cierra thought abuse was all she was and that was who she had become, but God had other plans for the pain she endured. From insecurities, to anxiety, depression, and suicidal thoughts, Cierra has survived, thrived, and become a victor! More determined than ever, Cierra has taken all that she has persevered through to teach others how to survive through the power of faith, prayer, and obedience to Christ, and in 2019, she founded the "I Survived It" ministry.

Professionally, Cierra works as a Patient Access Lead Specialist and oversees a team of 9 people. In ministry, she is a praise and worship leader, and speaker. In fall 2020, Cierra will be a part of the Dear Fear Volume 4 anthology, releasing her first published works.

Cierra enjoys singing, ministry, and spending time with her family and friends. She lives by the mantra "With God, nothing is impossible and all things are possible!"

JESSICA BROWN

Dear Fear,

For as long as I can remember you've shaken me to the very core of my existence. You made me feel as if I wasn't good enough, that I would always be misunderstood, and that no one would ever accept me. You've caused me to feel angry, rejected, abandoned, and just plain disgusted with myself. Because of you, fear, I've lived my entire life thinking everybody was out to get me. Who could want to be around me, to befriend me, to love me with all of my baggage? These are the things you've whispered to me. I've tried several times to kill myself because you popped up and told me I wouldn't be successful, so why even try? I can't believe I allowed you to control my mind for so long. Silly me!! But guess what? **THAT ENDS NOW!** I've decided to take my life back. My Daddy in Heaven has made me fearfully and wonderfully. I am worthy. I am beautiful. I am creative. I am intelligent. I am deserving of love. I am more than enough.

To be honest, I don't think I've ever been more excited to lose something before in my life. Fear, it's been real but it's time we break up. I know you hoped I failed time and time again but faith and failure cannot co-exist. Fear, you took full control of my past but you cannot have my future. Fear, I decree and declare that this is your exodus!

Goodbye Forever……Jess

Dear Fear, You Can't Have My Future

When I first started writing my story, I had the perfect way to jump into it. I was going to tell all about my painful experiences from a factual standpoint, how I felt I was the black sheep and I didn't deserve this or that. I was going to share how everyone did me wrong or how people left me. I was going to play the victim. It wasn't until after the Dear Fear Bootcamp that I realized that was not the purpose of me being here, and that was NOT going to set me or you free. This journey made me realize that I needed to release the emotions and stains of my pains so that I would not unintentionally pour them into my daughter, Aubrii Rose. She deserves a mother who is strong enough to realize her faults, deal with those things, and break down the bloodline barriers that could potentially stifle her path. I had to tear down that wall of having it all together. The reality is, I was a torn-up, broken mess inside. I know that victory begins with the truth! That was my truth, but it is not my now!

As you know before we talk about the testimony, we must talk about the tests. Let's start with childhood Jessica. Soon after my birth, my grandparents insisted on taking me back to Dothan with them to allow my mother to finish her degree. Looking back, here is where my first run-in with abandonment snuck in. I'm sure at the time she might have just been focused on the income of our family and not intentionally neglecting me. This issue would pop back up at age 24 soon after having my own child. I overheard my mother having a conversation that she had my daughter more than me, and seemed to be raising her. Trigger! The uncovering of a wound that had been patched over but not dealt with.

In September of 1994, my world got turned upside down. The man who I never saw sick or tired, my best friend who would watch cartoons until I got sleepy, was diagnosed with the big c. **CANCER.** My Superman found his Kryptonite and this poison quickly consumed him. At 6, I'm sure I didn't fully grasp the concept of death. I just knew they kept telling me my "Daddy" passed away. The last time I saw him was when I was saying goodbye, he was in a suit in a shiny box. I knew I would never see him pull up in his Buick with my cheeseburger kid meal or Snicker bar in his hand.

Who would have imagined that 6 short years later, history would repeat itself? I had just started to feel normal again. Normal didn't last long. Now, it was my granny's time. We took her back and forth to Birmingham to get the best treatment possible but it still wasn't enough. After a brain aneurysm, consistent seizures, and requiring a trach, she got tired and went to be with "Daddy" in 2001. I didn't have another set of grandparents I could just call on to try to fill this void. I was rejected by my father's parents at birth. According to the stories I've heard, my father's mother was disappointed with my father's choice to be with my mother. However, that's a truth that has yet to be uncovered. A conversation that's always been swept under the rug. If there is any truth to it, how could anyone mistreat an innocent child who did not ask to be here? If there is any truth to it, did my father not defend me?

As horrible as it all sounds, in my most recent moments of reflection, I began wondering how far down did the rejection and abandonment go in our family? As we all know those ugly generational cycles are the worst to break. 12-year-old Jess felt lost, confused, rejected, abandoned, and just plain not good enough!

At the time of granny's death, we had already moved back to Dothan into the home I grew up in. I can't lie, living with my parents alone was an adjustment. The focus was taken off of being caregivers to a "normal" life. During this transition to normalcy, I discovered I was a lot like my mama which more often than not resulted in arguments. In my adulthood, it was revealed that the version of "Daddy" who loved me so perfectly didn't do the same for her. My mama's version of him was a workaholic, the provider of the family who didn't have time for all the mushy love that I received (I guess this is what's meant by a grandparent's love is different). How ironic! "Daddy" worked all the time not leaving much time to love on my mama. My mama in turn leaves me to finish school and work, not leaving much time to love on me. Then there's me who finished school and immediately started picking up extra shifts not leaving much time to love on my daughter. Cycles!

When the referee of our fights(my father) was incarcerated, those same similarities of me and my mama allowed moments of bonding and made us inseparable. When I struggled to form and maintain friendships due to unhealed places in my life(but normally blamed the other party), she stepped right in and became my best friend and my human diary.

Fast forward to 2013, I left home in Dothan for Montgomery to attend college at ASU. While there, an old classmate from high school slid in my DM's, and the rest was history. He showed me things I'd never seen, took me places I'd never been, and loved me in a way that I felt secure. He filled a void that had been empty for a while. **Lesson: Never search for in a man the things that only God can fulfill.** With this man, a new life was formed but I felt so depressed. Before this pregnancy, I had three miscarriages. I was less than thrilled to repeat history especially with a man who I just knew I wanted to be with forever. In February 2014, the man I loved proposed to me. I was breaking the statistics y'all. I wasn't going to be a young black girl out here raising my baby alone, sis was about to get married! In March 2014, we welcomed the most beautiful baby girl into the world. For the first time in a very long time, I felt whole. I felt complete. I had purpose. How quickly that dialogue changed. By August of the same year, I was handing him back his engagement ring, packing my and baby girl's things back up, and heading back to Dothan with my parents. My fairytale love became a tale of the past.

Between the stress of my love story ending, the "I told you so's" and just the incredible pressures of being a new mommy, I was ready to end it all. Less than a month after my fairytale ending, I sent a round of text messages to the people that I loved saying my goodbyes. After ingesting a bottle of unknown pills, I laid there in the dark knowing it would be all over soon. Just as quickly as fear had stepped in and told me I wasn't good enough, Jesus called me out of that darkness and said **NOT NOW**, you are everything to me! He began to revive me, restore me, and send me help!

One of the ways God sent help was through my Uncle's wife. She gave me hope that after all I'd been through that something good could finally come out of this. She told me "when your granddaddy died, he left you with his mantle. You now have to break the generational curses off this family. When I first met you, I knew you were different but just couldn't put my finger on why until now. You endure so much because you have much work to do." I hadn't heard such heartfelt words about ME in so long. Fear had convinced me that I wasn't worthy to be seen. In that moment, fear lost. I realized that my pain had a purpose.

The spirits of rejection and abandonment attached themselves to me in hopes of snatching me from the will of my Father. Fear, you are manipulative. You knew if I felt unloved, unprotected, and unwanted by the people I loved suicide would present itself and the mantle would possibly die along with me. My daughter would be forced to feel every emotion that I had until that point. Ha, you gotta be quicker than that! Everything that fear tried didn't work!

It took me to age 30 to realize that my grandparents didn't abandon me, but they did help free me. They gave me access to the keys that would turn the locks to open doors to break generational curses. Without their passing, the mantle wouldn't have been passed down. I had to feel lost and confused like Elisha to reap the rewards of my Elijah. If nobody ever tells you this, let me tell you that you matter, your feelings matter, and your truth matters! The burden(s) that you are carrying right now are just the weight of the mantle that's on your life. You are not insignificant, you aren't a reject but instead you are a generational curse breaker. Tear down those strongholds! You aren't the dark sheep, you are the light that will uncover the dark secrets in your bloodline. Place your fears into the hands of our creator and He will transform them into fruit. Your nation will know you by the fruit that you bear!

I hope by reading my story that fear begins to lose its grip on you and you will join me in saying hey fear, you can't have my future because I am no longer the victim. I have the victory now!

Is there something in your life that you really want to do or is there something you are passionate about but haven't done because of fear? Name those things. Anything that has a name must submit to the highest name, Jesus.

_____

_____

_____

_____

What fears will you surrender so that you can make the impact you are called to make?

_____

_____

_____

_____

Bio:

Jessica Brown is a 31 year old amazing mother, nurse and lover of coffee and Christ. She is a front line worker sacrificing daily for our country in the midst of a pandemic. She currently resides in Dothan, AL. and is a member of Hines Chapel AME where she is submitted under the leadership of Pastor Paul Horn.

SHENEQUA JEFFERSON

Dear Fear,

As soon as I said "yes" you said "no"! Ever since I was a little girl you always made me feel unworthy and defenseless, but guess what? This time you lose. Why? Because once I gained the knowledge to know that God has given me the power to tread upon serpents, scorpions, and over all the power of the enemy, and that nothing by any means shall hurt me. (Luke 10:19) I have become fully aware of your deception, and every disguised tactic you operate in. I have realized that the dominion that was given to me by my Heavenly Father overpowers your existence.

I have inherited the rights to walk in Authority when it comes to my life, so as far as I am concerned you are illegal and you are trespassing. I now arrest you, and the chains you once placed on me that connected me to depression. I arrest you and the feeling of rejection! That curse has been destroyed. I am using those chains to detain you. I am now free and I am taking my life back. Your access to me has been denied. Expect more chains to be broken as I use my keys to help break others free. You thought you had a life sentence over me, but God has replaced my ashes for beauty! No more fear, no more doubt, no more depression, no more bondage, and no more strongholds. I am releasing prosperity, boldness, courage, transformation, and dignity over my life. I have taken back my confidence. In keeping God first I cannot, and will not fail. My NOW faith overpowers my PAST fear.

Signed:

Shenequa Jefferson

Dear Fear, You Can't Nullify My Forgiveness

Dear Judas,

You have been forgiven.

Signed,

Shenequa Branch

You may be thinking who is Judas? I'm sure you've encountered a Judas or two in your life. In fact, we all have. A Judas is someone who we allow to get close to us, someone who we allow in our personal space, yet the entire time their purpose was to deceive us. They leave you feeling like a fool, rejected, and unworthy. The betrayal incites the spirit of fear, which creeps in and convinces you that you are unloved, unwanted, and unsupported. Because of this, you shut down emotionally and you are left searching for anything to fill a void that Judas left. Before you met Judas, you were whole, and when Judas left, you were broken. Did your Judas Just come to mind?

The first time I encountered my Judas was at the age of five. It seemed like I had everything until I realized I was missing something. Growing up as a little girl with a strong single mother, and three siblings my mother was like a superwoman to me. I remember one day while playing with my cousin, a green car pulled into the yard. I noticed a man walking towards me, a man who I had never seen before. I began to wonder who this guy could be. It didn't take long to find out. He greeted me, and said, "hey I'm your dad". At five years old I didn't realize the impact those words were going to have on my life.

I accepted it as well as an offer for a happy meal. I mean what five year old was going to turn down a happy meal? I'm sure my mom wouldn't let me ride with a stranger so I went. Awkwardly riding in a car, with a man who says he was my father, left me in a state of excitement. I couldn't help but think "wow now I have a dad too"! On the way back home he told me how much he cared for me, and loved me. He assured me I would see him soon leaving me with expectations that he would return. Little did I know he wouldn't come back soon like he said he would. It seems like the Happy meal was the best part of that day(1995). I just didn't know it would have been the last one.

Meeting my father caused questions to arise that were never there. This led me into a very emotional conversation with my mom, and her telling me about how she and my father met. My mom told me how much of a blessing I was because she thought she could never have children again. At that moment I couldn't help but think if I'm such a blessing, why doesn't my father want me. How can he show up for one day and never come back? What did I do? What did I say? Is there something wrong with me? Every day I would wake up with the expectation of seeing that green car pull up again, hearing that deep male voice, but instead nothing.

The day I met my dad, my life changed. I had a new perspective on life. My innocence was shattered. The void was now visible, and I saw it everywhere I went. At school functions, at home, and church. I began to notice everyone else's father was there, except mine. I began to notice things I never noticed before.

My friends had two parents. Not me. Others were waiting for the ice cream truck after school but I was still waiting for that green car to pull up. It never showed. My grades began to go down, my attitude changed. The sweet girl with straight A's and full of life found herself suffering from selective mutism. I didn't understand how my life went from great to sitting in a counselor's office being evaluated, and monitored every week. I became overwhelmed with depression and in bondage with my emotions. I didn't realize this bondage would follow me for years to come.

I'll never forget the day I thought things were getting better for me. My friend was hosting a slumber party and was preparing to invite all of her friends. She was sharing with me how great her dad was, and I was excited to meet him. I patiently waited for the call to come through with my official invite. When the phone rang, there was nothing but disappointment on the other side. My friend said," I'm sorry Shenequa, my dad said you can't come." I asked why. She said, "because you're black." Her "amazing" dad that had never met me, uninvited me because I was black. I lost a friend that day, however, for me, it was another dad rejecting me. Another man rejected me before he ever knew WHO I was. Unforgiveness began to take over my life. I began to hate myself, my name, and question who I was. Why is it that me being me wasn't accepted or good enough? It hurts to know that you are giving your all, and it still isn't enough for others to stay.

The broken little girl "Shenequa" became the broken woman named "Renee". At the age of sixteen, my mom and I lost our home, car, and her Job. For me to finish school, and graduate without relocating, I had to live with my father. 11 years later and my dreams were finally coming true. Finally, he can see how great I am! It wasn't long before the dream life became a nightmare. My efforts of trying my best were always failures to him. I appreciated him for welcoming me into his home and providing for me, but there was no love. I dreamt of being his little princess, yet there was no crown. "I love yous" were replaced with "do better". Success stories were not failure stories. I resented my father for not being there seventeen years of my life. I began to replay moments of struggle with my mom, and with every thought, I resented him more.

Where was he when we sat in the dark? Where was he when the pantry was low? Why were you riding when we were walking? My desire as a little girl to build a bond with my father turned into a grudge called unforgiveness. I moved with him to mend the pieces, but instead, I felt broken again. Instead of healing from the pain, I dealt with it by learning how to save others to not focus on myself.

My cry for my father's attention led me on a path to search for love and attention in all the wrong places. Every date and every relationship I ever encountered were with men that I cared for more than they could ever care for me. Instead of owning my brokenness, and mistakes, I blamed My father for every guy who broke my heart. I knew I needed healing and I couldn't do it in my own will. At 22 years old, still broken and unable to forgive, I gave my life to Christ and that's where my healing started. One day I had taken the last heartbreak I could take. I remember for weeks laying in my apartment not wanting to get out of bed questioning if everything I had been through was for purpose or just for pain. I was contemplating my life, and what it would be like if I no longer existed. I cried out to God if he healed my heart, I would never put myself in a position to be hurt again. It wasn't only what I experienced with my father, but also what I put myself through.

I had to learn to forgive those who wronged me for my deliverance. I had to learn that everything that happened with my father wasn't my burden to carry. I had to learn that the decisions I made in life weren't all because of the ones who hurt me. I chose to stay the victim instead of the victor. The truth is I didn't know my worth. I didn't know the value of life. I had to learn why God created me the way he did. If you don't know why then it's easy to let life question your worth. It's easy for depression, oppression, suicide, poverty, and generational curses to run your life. It is the fear of the unknown that holds you back from being you, not everyone else. My leaders told me one day to read the book of Ruth and follow. I learned that although Ruth had faced unforeseen circumstances, she stayed busy.

She didn't look for love or the approval of man, and while she was busy she was being sustained and processed. While she may have felt burdened with the loss of her husband, she remained faithful, and busy instead of reasoning. I began to keep busy in my church striving to please Christ, and cherishing the agape love from my Heavenly Father. I decided to stop searching for love from others and seek the one who always loved me. The word of God tells us we are acquitted from everything including our past if we choose to repent of our old ways and strive in righteousness. We must learn how to exult and triumph in our troubles, and still rejoice despite the suffering.

Our maturity comes when our faith and integrity is tried, and we can still triumph instead of tapping out. (That's a word!) We must continue to glorify God the same as we did before the struggles. We must learn not to bow to circumstances, but stand until there is a solution. Forgive those who have wronged us. You don't need reconciliation to forgive someone. Remember Jesus was betrayed by Judas himself and yet he forgave him and still called him a friend. What Judas did was wrong but there was a purpose in the pain Jesus endured. Forgiveness clears our hearts in the eyes of the lord. How can God use us for purpose when we can't forgive as he has forgiven us? How could we ever minister to people when we haven't healed ourselves? I thank God for giving me spiritual parents who taught me how to deal with me and to seek healing for the wounds I carried. While in my brokenness God favored me. I was still bruised, yet God blessed me!.

A wise man that I know looked at me in a church service one day. He pointed at me and asked me if I wanted a husband. I was shaken. My mind said "no" but my heart cried "yes." He asked me to describe the husband I wanted. I named basic things like a good man with good credit. He instructed me to go home, pray, and describe the husband I wanted again. He instructed me to set my table for two every day and it would come to pass. I did so and six months later the man I prayed for came into my life. It wasn't just the fact that a man came into my life. It was the fact that God loved and favored me enough to give me something I never had, and something I longed for. True love and to be truly loved. I learned that for the empty void I carried to be filled, I had to seek the filler for who he truly was, and not just for what he could do for me. Our healing is, and will always be in prayer, fasting, and studying the word of God. It brings us deliverance day by day.

As for my earthly father, I began to understand why he made the choices he made. I saw his efforts. I'm thankful that we were able to move forward and build our relationship. Not only did God bless me to build a relationship with my father, but he also blessed me with a spiritual father, and gave me a husband too. If there is someone you need to forgive, whether it's a parent, an old friend, or a family member, forgive them.

Unforgiveness places strongholds on your life physically, mentally, and financially. It blocks your blessings and it affects your health. What you need from the Lord is laying dormant until you forgive. Most importantly forgive yourself for allowing the actions of someone else to hold you hostage from the life you deserve. We shouldn't allow the things we never had to hold us back from having it now. We must stop bearing crosses that were already defeated over 2,000 years ago. We can't live our life forever blaming others as the reason why we never succeeded.

We may have carried generational curses from our grandparents, but we have the opportunity to break them. There may have been doors that were once locked, but there is an opportunity for them to be opened. The fear that's holding you back can turn into just enough faith to push you forward. There is freedom in your forgiveness, and purpose in your pain. Don't change your identity to be accepted. Own who you are, and only change what stunts your growth. Don't reject you because you're being rejected by someone else. That's telling God we don't appreciate his creation. We must remember the stone that the builders rejected became the chief cornerstone. (Psalm 118:22). The "you" that you're rejecting, was designed to only be accepted by God, and to free others who are just like you. Yes it hurts, but what has pained you serves a purpose for your good. Remember, Judas is what pushed Jesus to his destiny. That's why it's important to forgive your Judas. Jesus wouldn't have been able to fulfill the prophecy without Judas' betrayal. Judas was one of Jesus twelve. It was the one closest to him that pushed the purpose. I can imagine if I had known in advance who would hurt me. I would have said no to that happy meal. But that one yes, the last happy meal, pushed me to destiny. Had I never forgave my Judas, I never would have known what I would be capable of overcoming. We have the power to press. there is revival in your forgiveness. Your hardship produces patience. My question to you now is this...have you forgiven your Judas? I'll go first.

Dear Dad,

It wasn't always you. It was me too. I forgive you.

Have you forgiven your Judas? Why or why not?

_____

_____

_____

_____

Most of the time the one you haven't forgiven has no idea how you truly feel. What would you say to them? Use this time to write a letter to this person to complete your forgiveness. Dear.... etc..

_____

_____

_____

_____

Bio:

Shenequa Jefferson is from Blakely Ga. however resides in Dothan Al. She attended Dothan High school and also Troy State University. She majored in Criminal Justice and Minored in Forensic science at Wallace college. She is a certified Independent broker of JTS Logistics solutions and served in Law enforcement for 5years for the Houston county sheriff's department. She served in the Nuclear Security department at Farley Nuclear power plant. She is also the leader of Mentor of Girl Talk at M.E.C. Dothan The word and Healing center. She is a Jovial worshipper of Jesus Christ! Locate Shenequa on all social media. Instagram @sheneJ90 & Facebook Shenequa Jefferson to see her New upcoming Business, Blog, and Book adventures!

KEEKEE LENNAY

Dear Fear,

I'm tired of having conversations with you. Why is it that whenever I feel like I am headed in the right direction you rear your ugly head? You can't fathom the dope person I am and have the potential to be so you show up in spaces you don't belong....or do you? Do you exist because in some weird way you bring out the best in me? Let's sit in that for a second. Let me paint the picture for you. I have a big idea, a life-changing opportunity, or a goal that I am close to reaching, and then BOOM here you come. Standing there with your big "aht aht" sign. It's almost like you don't want the world to see me. You don't want the world to see the real me. So you show your face and try to get in my way and you beat me down so good that I almost give up.

Then I rise.

I rise higher than I imagine. I do the unimaginable. I do the unthinkable. I master skills beyond my wildest dreams. The opportunity that was so big gets even bigger. And I can't help but think that because you had my back against the wall I worked harder. I felt like I needed to wrestle with you almost and the victory somehow became sweeter. In a fight with you for my voice, I began to speak louder and with more intention. I would stand toe to toe with you, enunciating every sound in the words that I spoke to show you that I wasn't scared of your existence and if you decided to attempt to interrupt my greatness that you would just have enjoyed the ride because even with interruption I was going to WIN!!!. So FEAR you tried it but I'm better at it. Always will be. Thank you for all you thought you were going to do to me and how you thought you would keep me silent, it made my voice ten times louder. Preciate Ya!

throws peace sign up and blow you a kiss

~Kee

Dear Fear,
You Can't Have My Perseverance

In Loving Memory of Barbara Ann Jones

Would you believe I completed this in the 9th hour? Yea, ya girl was ready to throw in the towel and walk away from this assignment. Understanding that procrastination is fear dressed up, I still convinced myself that I made the wrong choice answering THIS call. With running my business and dealing with the recent death of my grandmother I could not see myself writing anything. But then I got the message "Hey are you still in this with us?" from our Visionary Author. Now, this was not the first time I received this message, but this time in the 9th hour it meant something different for me. I couldn't ignore the call any longer. I began to think about all the women who could and would make magic in the 9th hour after reading how I did it. I thought about all the women who would slap fear in the face and commit to finishing something that mattered to them. I thought about all the women who would not give up because I chose not to. This story is for them.

I grew up a part of a blended family. I never met my biological father and my "stepfather" (we typically do not use this word but for reference, I did here) have always and will always treat me as his own. The reality is however, I never have felt apart of his family. I never felt like I "blended" well. Because of this, I always wanted to be "a part" of something. I longed for support, community, and collectiveness because I felt like it was everything I did not get as a child. And what does one do when there is a void or longing? They search for something to fill it. I was no different. My feelings of wanting unconditional love led me to my abuser. I met him and he paid zero attention to me in an intimate fashion, and I had no immediate interest in him. When he began to show me signs of security and support, that's when I fell. And boy did I fall hard. The problem with searching to fill a void is you usually fill it with things that are NOT good. This was my story. His support that I loved quickly turned into abuse, manipulation, and two of the worst years of my life.

But like most people who are being abused, I stayed. Why? Because I still craved a sense of community and comfort. I stayed in this relationship because I felt like even with all the crap, I could still count on him to be there for me. So, I stuck it out. I stuck it out when he physically harmed me. I stuck it out when he cheated on me. I stuck it out when he used words to hurt and fracture my self-esteem. I stuck it out because the fear of having no support crippled me.

If there was one good thing that came out of this toxic relationship, was that his cruel words led me to the scale. Seeing that number led me back to myself. The journey back to me gave me the confidence to love my body exactly where it was while creating a healthier temple for me to live in. While losing 80lbs was a major accomplishment, it was making the decision in the 9th hour to choose ME that became my biggest accomplishment from that relationship. When most would think they had no other choice but to endure abuse I decided in the last moments that I was worth more and I deserved more. I chose me. I no longer cared about the community and support. I chose me. I no longer cared about counting on him. I chose me. I no longer allowed fear to cripple me. I chose me.

After leaving my toxic relationship and losing weight I began the journey of looking for fulfillment. I knew corporate America was not my calling but if not corporate America then what? I was newly single with bills longer than my current paycheck and while I was free from that relationship, I still felt trapped. I had been drawn to a nutrition club called Nourish, which helped me on my journey and I realized my only peace was the time I spent there. I signed up to volunteer behind the bar for one hour a day to have some positivity in my life before heading to work. There I began to find what I was always looking for. Community and a place to belong. Although I only spent one hour there per day, it was enough to make the other hours of my day bearable. The nutrition club intrigued me, and I imagined having a space of my own like this to offer the community. I became a sponge. I soaked up all the knowledge that I could from my mentor with hopes of opening this healthy happy hangout spot for my community. I needed to open this haven and provide a space for the next Keekee who was just looking to belong. I was not paid hourly for my time, but I was given experience and training. Many people, including myself at times, called me crazy for showing up for this space the way that I did. I knew that Nourish gave me comfort when no one else did. This was my safe space, and I was indebted to it. I also felt in my gut that my time there would prepare me for something great. I wasn't wrong. A little over 5 years ago I walked into Nourish as a volunteer. Today I am the owner of the space that completely changed my life. I am now responsible for providing community and support all because I stuck it out and did not let fear win.

My goal is that my story encourages you to move beyond your quit. I want you to understand there is greatness that can come from the fourth quarter. As stated in the beginning I almost did not write this, but I would be doing myself and you a disservice if I did not share how removing fear and following my gut landed me a business and the pleasure of you reading my words. Fear gripped me and had me thinking my story did not matter and convinced me that I was alone in this when the whole time I had a group of women rooting for me. So I'm returning the favor. I am now rooting for you. Take heed to the girl who was once homeless, lived with three other roommates, and barely made enough money to cover her bills. Now that same girl owns a whole business. And the best and most rewarding part is the business I own gave me everything that I always knew I needed comfort and serenity and that is everything to me.

Have you ever wanted to quit something but for whatever reason you couldn't walk away? What kept you drawn to the task?

_____

_____

_____

_____

If you could be, do, or have anything in the world—what it be? What would you do? What would you want to have?

_____

_____

_____

_____

Bio:

Keekee Lennay is a health and nutrition entrepreneur in Raleigh NC. She is a Detroit MI native who fell in love with the easy living in Raleigh and never looked back. After leaving a toxic relationship and overcoming domestic violence she decided to take control over her health and life. She has successfully lost over 80lbs, ran a half marathon, and started implementing small changes to her lifestyle to be healthier and happier. Her mission in life is to show women that living a healthy lifestyle can be made simple and on your terms. She coaches girls to tap into their authentic self and love the body they live in. Her goal is to show women that "life after" a traumatic event can be fulfilling and magical. She is a lover of all things dance, good music, good vibes and Beyonce. You can always find her laughing uncontrollably and unapologetically loud and participating in her favorite sport: cheering on women to do whatever they set their mind to.

TIANA PATRICE

Dear Fear, You Can't STOP My Healing

"Baby, stop running back and forth to that door"

— Grandma Ruthie Lee

"I'm just waiting on my daddy to come back"

— Young Patrice

It's impossible to tell the end of a story, without the beginning. I don't mean the surface beginning with sunshine and rainbows, accolades, and "as seen in". I mean the ugly truths that for years we try to hide with beautiful smiles, careers, and glittery brands. The ugly truths that many of us skip over once we find a version of success that doesn't mirror where we have been.

For many of us, the beginning of a barren place begins in childhood from unhealed wounds. If we ever stop to peel back the layers of the onion we call life, we will find seeds of insecurities, doubts, and self-sabotaging beliefs that were planted before we even had a chance to know who we were.

Those seeds that were planted grew weeds that attempted to destroy the innocence of the nutrient-rich soil God created us from. These weeds grew roots that were never intended to reap a harvest, yet because these areas of our lives were left unchecked, unplucked, and weeded out we now have a society of adults living lives with withered fruit, putting price tags on it and calling it success.

Because we have allowed our past, our traumas, our brokenness to dictate our lives, raise our children and run our businesses, we have unhealed leaders pouring out of barren places and killing with each pour. We have unhealed parents raising children in the same cycles they were forced to live in. We have influencers, influencing from a place of pain calling it purpose. We have CEOs and executives running big corporate brands with unchecked privilege screaming All Lives Matter while blatantly disregarding the lives of the ones monetizing their wealth.

So how do we kill the seeds planted by the enemy?

First, we identify the lie, and we combat it with truth, prayer, and worship. The bible tells us in *John 8:32 "Ye shall know the TRUTH and the TRUTH shall set you free"*. This means that to combat the lies of the enemy we must first know the truth. Not what man says, not what Satan says, but what God says about us!

Let's meet young Patrice.

You may have heard the story before. You know, the story of the daddyless daughter looking for love in all the wrong places. Searching to fill voids created by one man, by the arms of many. My story is not much different.

Raised by a single mom and a praying grandmother, I was bred to work hard, grind non stop, take care of myself, and make sure that I owned the table. #Period My grandmother's position was for all of her girls to *"go to college, learn to get your own so that what a man brings to the table isn't all you have to eat".* Because of the era she was raised in and the struggles she experienced in marriage, the root of her teaching was *"you never want to be the woman that can't leave because you don't have anything. At that point he has all control, can do what he wants, and all you can say is wash up before you come to dinner"*

Say less, Granny.

Seed. Planted.

Raised in part from versions of their pain, I learned to be an independent woman and not trust men long before Lil' Boosie came out. Mix in growing up with a father whose presence was dependent on convenience and favorable conditions....chileee my weeds were out of control. Gardened by his absence and watered by his lies, every seed took root and entered another area of my life. The lies of "I'll be back" planted seeds of "I didn't choose you, you aren't enough, you aren't worthy of my time, there is always something better than you…" What could a fetus have done that was so bad for him not to want to stay?

You see, the truth is the divorce didn't happen in 2019. I'd be lying if I said that the record was chopped, screwed, and rejected during the divorce. The reality is it was a record that had been playing for 30 years of my life. From the days of waiting at the window for daddy to come back to the many failed situationships before. Same record, different track.

Another man.

Another broken promise.

And in my adult age, another thing I allowed.

Yet another feeling of never being enough or worthy for someone to stay. The unhealed 15 year old was proved to be right yet again. *Everyone that loves you…leaves you.* What was a vow to something that was already expired? For fatherless daughters, we are bred to "run to doors" in expectation of something or someone to be there. For many of us, the thing waiting at the door mirrored the voids we carried and the love we longed for but weren't designed to carry us. #Message

The problem with the door is that instinctively it creates a false hope and plants a seed called disappointment when hope doesn't translate to reality. We then create a covenant with the door of rejection and abandonment and a soul tie with never being enough.

Another seed. Another weed.

Dang, I should've stopped running to that door.

Because I wasn't healed 30-year-old Tiana walked down the aisle, but 15-year-old Tiana said "I do". When we don't confront the door and burn it down, we allow things that are familiar with this brokenness to have access to our purpose at any time. Thus, marrying situationships and attempting to turn them into lifetimes.

Walls of distrust were built before I was 8. Insecurities of never being enough became my truth before I was 10. By the time I was 13, I was a teenager with a mission to not let anyone get close enough to hurt me so I quickly learned how to control the narrative.

How many of you can relate with this?

You learned to hurt before you got hurt, leave before you were left, and hide how much you truly cared. When dating, I never stayed long with those that truly had my best interest at heart. That was too easy. I wasn't conditioned for easy. I was conditioned for struggle. (Who caught that) I never chose those that chose me, I chose the ones that didn't have the capability to fully choose me back. (Cute things that were also broken.) A. Whole. Word.

Before we continue, I want you to do a quick self-inventory.

Take some time and ask yourself, what is your door made of? Is it rejection, abandonment, fear? When is the last time you actually confronted it? Are you connecting to people, places, and things out of alignment with your assignment because your door is wide open? And if so, what do you believe will happen if you never lean into God's truth and shut it?

Seriously, pause for a second and think about some situations you have gotten into because you didn't unlearn the lies from your childhood. Think about the relationships you entered into because you weren't healed. The bedroom aisles you went down because you positioned your worth in the arms of another. Think about the lies you believed because you weren't abiding in Christ.

Self inventories are never fun, they require that you are open and honest with yourself, so that true healing and deliverance can occur. They require that you fully surrender, acknowledge, and identify the barren places in your life. *Again, how do we kill the weed?* With Truth, Prayer, and Worship.

> *"And all things, whatsoever ye shall ask in prayer, believing, ye shall receive."*
>
> -Matthew 21:22

Two years ago as God really began to pull me into my purposed place he aligned me under the leadership of my Apostle, Paul Horn, and provided me with a safe place to grow and learn true servitude. (Interesting fact, God called me under this leadership before my engagement, but because I wanted to submit to my will, I didn't answer the call until 1 week AFTER I said "I do") I remember sitting in bible study one evening and Pastor Horn told us, "One of the most powerful prayers you can pray is Lord, show me, me." Hmm, that seemed simple enough. So I did. When I tell you, God opened the floodgates and began to show me childhood wounds, the roots of them, and more.

When God brings something up, he wants it to come out.

As God began to reveal and snatch up my weeds, I had to deal with the places in my life that were barren. I had to deal with abandonment and rejection. I had to deal with the thoughts of not being enough. I had to deal with trust issues. I had to deal with the independent woman. I had to deal with the lies of the enemy.

I had to DEAL.

You can't heal until you DEAL with YOU! God began to prune me, and speak to the broken areas. He began to silence the unhealed 15-year-old with love. My perspective began to change. I took responsibility and accountability for the areas of my life that I CHOSE to enter into situations out of God's will.

I accepted God's truth.

I am LOVED. I am CHOSEN. I am ENOUGH. I am POSSIBLE. I formed a relationship with him. I learned to rest in his presence. I worshiped in spirit and in truth. I gave him access to all of me. Not just the glittery parts, but the ugly parts that I covered up as a boss.

Every moment God "showed me, me", I would pray: *"God remove it. I don't want it. God minister to it. I don't need it. God heal it. I want out. God overflow into that voided place I just want you"* And he did. Over and Over again. There is power in prayer! There is nothing you are experiencing that God doesn't understand. There is no broken place that God can't mend. There is no lie of the enemy that his truth won't demolish. There is no hurt place that God can't heal.

I am the proof!

This is weed killing season! I declare that the cycles of broken things are breaking now! In Jesus Name…Amen!

BIO:

Tiana Patrice is a mother and woman of God on a mission to redefine what it means to be fearless. She is the founder of The fearLESS Experience, where Kingdom meets the marketplace on the other side of fear. Hailed as the "fearLESS Activator", Tiana believes it's not enough to simply face your fear and rise. But you must Activate Your fear.LESS by doing the work to clip the root. Because of this, Tiana is on assignment to break generational strongholds of fear, and help leaders breakthrough to win on purpose, in purpose.

In her best-selling book series *Dear Fear*, Tiana partners with leaders from across the globe to create blueprints of what it looks like to acknowledge and take action against your fear of failure, success, possibilities, disappointment, and speak the language of Victory! When you connect with Tiana whether online, in person, or in reading one of her best selling books, you will see why audiences from all over the globe are committed to learning her strategies of how to strengthen their faith muscles and live their best life on the other side of fear.

Tiana has a natural ability to motivate, transform and minister to the core or her audiences while helping them identify, acknowledge, and take action on their fear-all while simultaneously helping them strengthen their relationship with God. Her energetic approach with easy to understand, thought-provoking and relatable messages help leaders tap into their core, find and clip the root of what's keeping them from their success. Her messages have been seen, read, and heard on multiple media outlets such as Forbes Women Under 30, ABC, CBS, Huffington Post and you can find The fearLESS Experience in more than 15 states and 3 countries.

"In this season we can't afford to let fear win. Our destiny, and those who we are called to lead, depends on us combatting our fear with faith. Now isn't the time to be afraid, now is the time to strengthen your faith and do the things God is calling you to do...and to heal because that's the mandate" *dearfearbook.com*

www.ingramcontent.com/pod-product-compliance
Lightning Source LLC
Chambersburg PA
CBHW070910160426
43193CB00011B/1414